Valerius Antias and Caesar

This little gem of a thesis by Carl Zohren, first published in 1910, was discovered by Laura Knight-Jadczyk during her research into the Roman Empire, and is now translated from German into English for the first time.

Historian and philologist Luciano Canfora said about Caesar: "When they killed him, his assassins did not realize that they had eliminated the best and most far-sighted mind of their class." This is the problem. According to all the history we are taught, Julius Caesar was a power-mad wannabe-king who destroyed Gaul and then the Roman Republic, and his assassination was a noble and justified act. That is how it is sold to us, at least. But a careful reading of the sources reveals something quite different.

Our problem lies in the fact that most of what we know – or think we know – about Caesar and those times, comes from his enemies. In Cicero, his most prolific contemporary, we see Caesar through the eyes of one of the most repulsive characters Rome ever produced. But the problem goes beyond Cicero; it is historians and historiography in general, and Valerius Antias, the main topic of this little book, was one of the chief architects of the deception. His work provided the justification Caesar's murderers needed to go down in history as Rome's saviors. But the truth is something completely different.

Dissertation

Valerius Antias and Caesar

CARL ZOHREN

1910

Red Pill Press

Copyright © 1910 Carl Zohren, Heinsberg, Rheinland.

Dissertation for the attainment of the doctorate at the Hohe Philosophische und Naturwissenschaftliche Fakultät, Königliche Universität Münster. Approbated May 7th, 1910. Faculty director: Prof. Dr. Kroll. Referent: Geheimer Regierungsrat Prof. Dr. Seeck. Published by Aktien-Gesellschaft für Verlag und Druckerei Der Westfale, Münster.

Translated from German into English by Michael Franzl in 2013. Translation edited by Laura Knight-Jadczyk. Foreword, commentary and additional footnotes by Laura Knight-Jadczyk. English translations of Latin and Greek quotations have been added into the text by the editor.

Republished by Red Pill Press in 2014.
http://www.redpillpress.com
Edition 1
ISBN 978-1-897244-91-3

Contents

Introduction 7

Acknowledgements 29

Antias and Caesar 31

Introduction

This little gem of a thesis was discovered during my research for an upcoming volume about the Roman Empire – part of my *Secret History of the World* series. After reading numerous studies of the life of Julius Caesar, Caesar's own writings, the ancient historians, recent historians, books and papers about historiography and who we can and cannot trust among the ancients and why and on and on and on, there was still, for me, this gigantic problem that was defined in a very short statement at the end of historian and philologist Luciano Canfora's *Julius Caesar: The People's Dictator*:

> When they killed him his assassins did not realize that they had eliminated the best and most far-sighted mind of their class.[1]

This was the problem. All the history we are taught says that Caesar was a power-mad wannabe-king who destroyed Gaul and then the Roman Republic, and his heirs fought over who would succeed him, Octavian won and became Augustus, but that was cool because he was a great guy and treated the senate well, and a later emperor, Constantine, saved Christianity, so aren't we glad they murdered Caesar? Sorry for the run-on sentence, but that is how the thing is sold to us. But a careful reading of the sources revealed something quite different. Classicist Arthur Kahn, who devoted 12 years to an in-depth study of Caesar, writes:

> Caesar recognized and warned that civil war would ravage the empire if he was killed, but the self-proclaimed champions of liberty and defenders of the constitution, the subversive-hunters, the praters of piety, of patriotism and of the ancestral virtues were prepared to pull down the world if their outmoded privileges were not restored.
> ...
> The difference between Caesar and the Ciceros and the Catos of his day and of all subsequent times is that unlike them Caesar

---
[1]Canfora, *Julius Caesar: The People's Dictator*, p. 348.

saw society as an integrity in motion; he was not confused by the apparent disconnection among social, economic, political and cultural developments. Thus he did not vacillate from week to week or even day to day in his judgments, and he was able both to evolve grandiose plans and to effect them. ... No one of his day sensed the future as he did or explored as many aspects of life experience, testing the limits of human capacities and seeking, in effect, to compel the world to adapt itself to his personal vision and aspirations. ... he sought to accomplish in his [lifetime] what, in fact, was to require generations. ...

... Ever conscious of the corruption that threatens men commanding absolute power, he disdained to enforce conformity through repression, rejected terror as a political weapon, refused to be alarmed by rumors, scorned the use of informers and despised the hunting of "subversives." Though harried into short temper [on occasion] and badgered by fools, he remained Caesar to the moment of his death. A man of extraordinary complexity, he possessed a penetrating intelligence coupled with a universal curiosity, an unyielding will and inexhaustible energy as well as an exuberance about the dynamic variety in life. As a foe he proved fierce and cunning, yet with an irresistible charm and a trenchant wit he captivated (and still captivates) even his enemies. ...

Caesar is the greatest personality of the thousand years of Roman history. Rightfully do we continue to commemorate him in the seventh month of the year.[2]

How could it be that Caesar, the "greatest mind of Rome", the greatest personality of possibly the last three thousand years (or more), who had done so much for so many – as was patently clear even via the hostile evidence of his opponents, mainly Cicero – could be assassinated by so-called "advocates of freedom"? And after that assassination, years of war went on and on, followed by the acceptance of exactly what they claimed to be rejecting in Caesar: a monarchy (in all but name)? And worse, how could it be that we have sustained this view for over 700 years since the rediscovery of the historical texts about ancient Rome?

The reason begins with Cicero:

All honest men killed Caesar ... some lacked design, some courage,

---

[2]Kahn, *The Education of Julius Caesar: A Biography, a Reconstruction*, pp. 450–3.

some opportunity: none lacked the will.[3]

No bigger lie has ever been propagated and our problem lies in the fact that most of what we know – or think we know – about Caesar and those times, comes from Cicero: we see Caesar through the eyes of one of the most repulsive characters Rome ever produced. But the problem goes beyond Cicero; it is historians and historiography in general, and Valerias Antias, the main topic of this little book, was one of the chief architects of the deception.

Notes about the organization of this translation and subsequent scholarships

Antias and Caesar by German historian Carl Zohren, which is translated here by Michael Franzl, is augmented by additional footnotes that will help the lay reader to orient him or herself, as well as inclusion within the text of some of the material alluded to by the author but not included by him since it was expected that scholars would be familiar with them. Further, the Latin and Greek excerpts that scholars are expected to be able to read themselves, have been augmented by translations, usually from the Loeb editions of the various works. If that is not the case, it will be noted. In some few cases, there are no translations and so some I have translated myself, others have been translated by Harrison Koehli or Irini Gregoriou. I've re-organized the text slightly as well, moving the last paragraph to the beginning, and the reader will notice that it references the great Theodor Mommsen as the inspiration. Again for the lay reader, I'm going to include Mommsen's famous re-evaluation of Julius Caesar as well as his remarks about Antias that are referred to in this thesis.

But first, let me point out that the issue discussed in Zohren's thesis here is one of continuing interest and dispute. The majority of scholars continue to accept the idea that Antias was an earlier writer than Cicero, in the face of the growing support for the later dating in the 40s BC, either during Caesar's dictatorship or after his assassination.

T. J. Cornell, Emeritus professor of Ancient History at the University of Manchester, a student of the highly esteemed Arnaldo Momigliano,

---

[3] Cicero, *Philippica*, 2.29.

argues weakly, in my opinion, for sustaining the earlier date.[4]

On the other side, T. P. Wiseman, Emeritus professor of the University of Exeter, educated at Baliol College, Oxford, and Fellow of the British Academy, notes that there are enough shared "Valerian Elements" in twelve well-known episodes of early Roman History to demonstrate that they are the work of one author who was writing between the time of the Catilinarian Conspiracy of 63 BC, and Cicero's rewriting of the Brutus in 46 BC.[5] In a review of Wiseman's Remembering the Roman People (2009), Mary Beard commented on Wiseman's methodology in trying to tease out a view of Roman popularist politics from elite-dominated sources:

> To find what he is looking for, Wiseman must read the sources against the grain, searching out hints of a different view of events, and looking for the cracks in the conservative story through which a glimpse of a popular tradition might be seen. He must look beyond the accounts of surviving ancient authors to the alternative versions that they were (consciously or unconsciously) concealing. In doing this, he not only depends on a rare familiarity with Roman literature, from the mainstream to its remotest byways, but also on a capacity for bold historical speculation that takes him right to the edge of (and in some cases beyond) what the surviving evidence can reliably tell us.[6]

Meanwhile, Gary Forsythe, Professor of History at Texas Tech, former Fellow of the School of Historical Study at the Institute for Advanced Studies in Princeton, author of *A Critical History of Early Rome: From Prehistory to the First Punic War*,[7] after a careful evaluation of the clues, also proposes in a later work,[8] that Antias was a Ciceronian era author. He suggests that it would have taken Antias 25 to 30 years to have completed his entire work (which was reportedly massive), starting around 70 BC and finishing up around 40 BC. Forsythe's reconstruction of Antias's

---

[4] Cornell, *Fragments of the Roman Historians*, pp. 293-304.
[5] "Valerius Antias and the Palimpsest of History" Wiseman, *Roman drama and Roman history*, pp. 75-89.
[6] Beard, "Spinning Caesar's murder: Putting the ideology – and the people – back into our understanding of Roman political life".
[7] Forsythe, *A Critical History of Early Rome: From Prehistory to the First Punic War*.
[8] Gorman, Robinson, and Graham, *Oikistes: Studies in Constitutions, Colonies, and Military Power in the Ancient World, Offered in Honor of A.J. Graham*.

organization of his work ends up being one of the most cogent pictures of Antias showing, by comparison with Livy, that Antias wrote a more expanded coverage of the early Republic. I would even like to suggest that it is altogether possible that Antias had time to edit his early history to fulfill the needs of the post-assassination period exactly as Zohren proposes in this book.

It should be noted that Antias' work has survived only in fragments though it was the fullest and longest work of its kind at the time it was written. His history wasn't preserved because it was said to be stylistically awful, though it was utilized by later historians which propagated many of his fabrications and inventions. Ernst Badian, late professor of history and classics at Harvard, said that Antias represented the "nadir of historiography."[9]

There were many works that did not survive the manuscript bottleneck of the collapse of the Roman Empire and the suppression of pagan history and literature by Christianity. The two histories that might be most regretted would be those of Asinius Pollio and L. Cornelius Balbus, both of whom were close associates of Julius Caesar. A fragment here and there are all that is left to give us clues that what has been preserved may be not just biased, but often completely fabricated.

---

[9]Badian, *Studies in Greek and Roman History.*

From Mommsen's famous *History of Rome*, chapter XI, excerpts:

On Caesar

The new monarch of Rome, the first ruler over the whole domain of Romano-Hellenic civilization, Gaius Julius Caesar, was in his fifty-sixth year (born 12 July 652? [102 BC?]) when the battle at Thapsus, the last link in a long chain of momentous victories, placed the decision as to the future of the world in his hands. Few men have had their elasticity so thoroughly put to the proof as Caesar – the sole creative genius produced by Rome, and the last produced by the ancient world, which accordingly moved on in the path that he marked out for it until its sun went down. ...

If in a nature so harmoniously organized any one aspect of it may be singled out as characteristic, it is this – that he stood aloof from all ideology and everything fanciful. As a matter of course, Caesar was a man of passion, for without passion there is no genius; but his passion was never stronger than he could control. He had had his season of youth, and song, love, and wine had taken lively possession of his spirit; but with him they did not penetrate to the inmost core of his nature. ...

Caesar was thoroughly a realist and a man of sense; and whatever he undertook and achieved was pervaded and guided by the cool sobriety which constitutes the most marked peculiarity of his genius. To this he owed the power of living energetically in the present, undisturbed either by recollection or by expectation; to this he owed the capacity of acting at any moment with collected vigour, and of applying his whole genius even to the smallest and most incidental enterprise; to this he owed the many-sided power with which he grasped and mastered whatever understanding can comprehend and will can compel; to this he owed the self-possessed ease with which he arranged his periods as well as projected his campaigns; to this he owed the "marvelous serenity" which remained steadily with him through good and evil days; to this he owed the complete independence, which admitted of no control by favourite or by mistress, or even by friend. It resulted, moreover, from this clearness of judgment that Caesar never formed to himself illusions regarding the power of fate and the ability of man; in his case the friendly veil was lifted up, which conceals from man the inadequacy of his working. Prudently as he laid his plans and considered all possibilities, the feeling was never absent from his breast that in all things fortune, that is to say accident, must bestow success; and with this may be connected the circumstance that he so often played a desperate game with destiny, and in particular again and again hazarded his person with daring indifference. As indeed occasionally men of predominant sagacity betake themselves to a pure game of hazard, so there was in Caesar's rationalism a point at which it came in some measure into contact with mysticism. ...

Gifts such as these could not fail to produce a statesman. From early youth, accordingly, Caesar was a statesman in the deepest sense of the term, and his aim was the highest which man is allowed to propose to himself – the political, military, intellectual, and moral regeneration of his own deeply decayed nation, and of the still more deeply decayed Hellenic nation intimately akin to his own. The hard school of thirty years' experience changed his views as to the means by which this aim was to be reached; his aim itself remained the same in the times of his hopeless humiliation and of his unlimited plenitude of power, in the times when as demagogue and conspirator he stole towards it by paths of darkness, and in those when, as joint possessor of the supreme power and then as monarch, he worked at his task in the full light of day before the eyes of the world. All the measures of a permanent kind that proceeded from him at the most various times assume their appropriate places in the great building-plan. We cannot therefore properly speak of isolated achievements of Caesar; he did nothing isolated.

With justice men commend Caesar the orator for his masculine eloquence, which, scorning all the arts of the advocate, like a clear flame at once enlightened and warmed. With justice men admire in Caesar the author the inimitable simplicity of the composition, the unique purity and beauty of the language. With justice the greatest masters of war of all times have praised Caesar the general, who, in a singular degree disregarding routine and tradition, knew always how to find out the mode of warfare by which in the given case the enemy was conquered, and which was thus in the given case the right one; who with the certainty of divination found the proper means for every end; who after defeat stood ready for battle ... and ended the campaign invariably with victory; who managed that element of warfare, the treatment of which serves to distinguish military genius from the mere ordinary ability of an officer – the rapid movement of masses – with unsurpassed perfection, and found the guarantee of victory not in the massiveness of his forces but in the celerity of their movements, not in long preparation but in rapid and daring action even with inadequate means. But all these were with Caesar mere secondary matters; he was no doubt a great orator, author, and general, but he became each of these merely because he was a consummate statesman.

The soldier more especially played in him altogether an accessory part, and it is one of the principal peculiarities by which he is distinguished from Alexander, Hannibal, and Napoleon, that he began his political activity not as an officer, but as a demagogue. According to his original plan he had purposed to reach his object, like Pericles and Gaius Gracchus, without force of arms, and throughout eighteen years he had as leader of the popular party moved exclusively amid political plans and intrigues–until, reluctantly convinced of the necessity for a military support, he, when already forty years of age, put himself at the head of an army. It was natural that he should even afterwards remain still more statesman than general ...

The task of the statesman is universal in its nature like Caesar's genius; if he undertook things the most varied and most remote one from another, they had all without exception a bearing on the one great object to which with infinite fidelity and consistency he devoted himself; and of the manifold aspects and directions of his great activity he never preferred one to another. Although a master of the art of war, he yet from statesmanly considerations did his utmost to avert civil strife and, when it nevertheless began, to earn laurels stained as little as possible by blood. Although the founder of a military monarchy, he yet, with an energy unexampled in history, allowed no hierarchy of marshals or government of praetorians to come into existence. If he had a preference for any one form of services rendered to the state, it was for the sciences and arts of peace rather than for those of war ...

The most remarkable peculiarity of his action as a statesman was its perfect harmony. In reality all the conditions for this most difficult of all human functions were united in Caesar. A thorough realist, he never allowed the images of the past or venerable tradition to disturb him; for him nothing was of value in politics but the living present and the law of reason, just as in his character of grammarian he set aside historical and antiquarian research and recognized nothing but on the one hand the living – *usus loquendi* – and on the other hand the rule of symmetry. A born ruler, he governed the minds of men as the wind drives the clouds, and compelled the most heterogeneous natures to place themselves at his service – the plain citizen and the rough subaltern, the genteel matrons of Rome and the fair princesses of Egypt and Mauretania, the brilliant cavalry-officer and the calculating banker. His talent for organization was marvelous; no statesman has ever compelled alliances, no general has ever collected an army out of unyielding and refractory elements with such decision, and kept them together with such firmness, as Caesar displayed in constraining and upholding his coalitions and his legions; never did regent judge his instruments and assign each to the place appropriate for him with so acute an eye.

He was monarch; but he never played the king. Even when absolute lord of Rome, he retained the deportment of the party-leader; perfectly pliant and smooth, easy and charming in conversation, complaisant towards every one, it seemed as if he wished to be nothing but the first among his peers. Caesar entirely avoided the blunder into which so many men otherwise on an equality with him have fallen, of carrying into politics the military tone of command; however much occasion his disagreeable relations with the senate gave for it, he never resorted to outrages ... Caesar was monarch; but he was never seized with the giddiness of the tyrant. He is perhaps the only one among the mighty ones of the earth, who in great matters and little never acted according to inclination or caprice, but always without exception according to his duty as ruler, and who, when he looked back on his life, found doubtless erroneous calculations to deplore, but no false step of passion to regret. ...

He is, in fine, perhaps the only one of those mighty ones, who has preserved to the end of his career the statesman's tact of discriminating between the possible and the impossible, and has not broken down in the task which for greatly gifted natures is the most difficult of all – the task of recognizing, when on the pinnacle of success, its natural limits. What was possible he performed, and never left the possible good undone for the sake of the impossible better, never disdained at least to mitigate by palliatives evils that were incurable. But where he recognized that fate had spoken, he always obeyed. Alexander on the Hypanis, Napoleon at Moscow, turned back because they were compelled to do so, and were indignant at destiny for bestowing even on its favourites merely limited successes; Caesar turned back voluntarily on the Thames and on the Rhine; and thought of carrying into effect even at the Danube and the Euphrates not unbounded plans of world-conquest, but merely well-considered frontier-regulations.

Such was this unique man, whom it seems so easy and yet is so infinitely difficult to describe. His whole nature is transparent clearness; and tradition preserves more copious and more vivid information about him than about any of his peers in the ancient world. Of such a personage our conceptions may well vary in point of shallowness or depth, but they cannot be, strictly speaking, different; to every not utterly perverted inquirer the grand figure has exhibited the same essential features, and yet no one has succeeded in reproducing it to the life. The secret lies in its perfection. In his character as a man as well as in his place in history, Caesar occupies a position where the great contrasts of existence meet and balance each other. Of mighty creative power and yet at the same time of the most penetrating judgment; no longer a youth and not yet an old man; of the highest energy of will and the highest capacity of execution; filled with republican ideals and at the same time born to be a king; a Roman in the deepest essence of his nature, and yet called to reconcile and combine in himself as well as in the outer world the Roman and the Hellenic types of culture – Caesar was the entire and perfect man.

Caesar was a perfect man just because he more than any other placed himself amidst the currents of his time, and because he more than any other possessed the essential peculiarity of the Roman nation – practical aptitude as a citizen – in perfection: for his Hellenism in fact was only the Hellenism which had been long intimately blended with the Italian nationality. But in this very circumstance lies the difficulty, we may perhaps say the impossibility, of depicting Caesar to the life. As the artist can paint everything save only consummate beauty, so the historian, when once in a thousand years he encounters the perfect, can only be silent regarding it. For normality admits doubtless of being expressed, but it gives us only the negative notion of the absence of defect; the secret of nature, whereby in her most finished manifestations normality and individuality are combined, is beyond expression. Nothing is left for us but to deem those fortunate who beheld this perfection, and to gain some faint conception of it from the reflected lustre which rests imperishably on the works that were the creation of this great nature. These also, it is true, bear the stamp of the time. The Roman hero himself stood by the side of his youthful Greek predecessor not merely as an equal, but as a superior ... With reason therefore the delicate poetic tact of the nations has not troubled itself about the unpoetical Roman, and on the other hand has invested the son of Philip with all the golden lustre of poetry, with all the rainbow hues of legend. But with equal reason the political life of the nations has during thousands of years again and again reverted to the lines which Caesar drew; and the fact, that the peoples to whom the world belongs still at the present day designate the highest of their monarchs by his name, conveys a warning deeply significant and, unhappily, fraught with shame. ...

... Caesar came not to begin, but to complete. The plan of a new polity suited to the times, long ago projected by Gaius Gracchus, had been maintained by his adherents and successors with more or less of spirit and success, but without wavering. Caesar, from the outset and as it were by hereditary right the head of the popular party, had for thirty years borne aloft its banner without ever changing or even so much as concealing his colours; he remained democrat even when monarch; as he accepted without limitation, apart of course from the preposterous projects of Catilina and Clodius, the heritage of his party; as he displayed the bitterest, even personal, hatred to the aristocracy and the genuine aristocrats; and as he retained unchanged the essential ideas of Roman democracy, viz. alleviation of the burdens of debtors, transmarine colonization, gradual equalization of the differences of rights among the classes belonging to the state, emancipation of the executive power from the senate: his monarchy was so little at variance with democracy, that democracy on the contrary only attained its completion and fulfilment by means of that monarchy. For this monarchy was not the Oriental despotism of divine right, but a monarchy such as Gaius Gracchus wished to found ... the representation of the nation by the man in whom it puts supreme and unlimited confidence. ...

... Caesar's work was necessary and salutary, not because it was or could be fraught with blessing in itself, but because – with the national organization of antiquity, which was based on slavery and was utterly a stranger to republican-constitutional representation, and in presence of the legitimate urban constitution which in the course of five hundred years had ripened into oligarchic absolutism – absolute military monarchy was the copestone logically necessary and the least of evils. ...

... Little was finished; much even was merely begun. Whether the plan was complete, those who venture to vie in thought with such a man may decide; we observe no material defect in what lies before us – every single stone of the building enough to make a man immortal, and yet all combining to form one harmonious whole. Caesar ruled as king of Rome for five years and a half, not half as long as Alexander; in the intervals of seven great campaigns, which allowed him to stay not more than fifteen months altogether in the capital of his empire, he regulated the destinies of the world for the present and the future, from the establishment of the boundary-line between civilization and barbarism down to the removal of the pools of rain in the streets of the capital, and yet retained time and composure enough attentively to follow the prize-pieces in the theatre and to confer the chaplet on the victor with improvised verses. The rapidity and self-precision with which the plan was executed prove that it had been long meditated thoroughly and all its parts settled in detail; but, even thus, they remain not much less wonderful than the plan itself. The outlines were laid down and thereby the new state was defined for all coming time; the boundless future alone could complete the structure. So far Caesar might say, that his aim was attained; and this was probably the meaning of the words which were sometimes heard to fall from him – that he had "lived enough." But precisely because the building was an endless one, the master as long as he lived restlessly added stone to stone, with always the same dexterity and always the same elasticity busy at his work, without ever overturning or postponing, just as if there were for him merely a to-day and no to-morrow. Thus he worked and created as never did any mortal before or after him; and as a worker and creator he still, after well nigh two thousand years, lives in the memory of the nations – the first, and withal unique, Imperator Caesar. ...

The next extract deals with the historians of Rome referenced in the thesis by Carl Zohren and historiography in general. It is probably these remarks that prompted the analysis of Antias and his campaign to defame Caesar and protect the assassins.

Mommsen's *History of Rome*, chapter XII, excerpts:

Historical Composition – Sisenna

The critical writing of history, after the manner in which the Attic authors wrote the national history in their classic period and in which Polybius wrote the history of the world, was never properly developed in Rome. Even in the field most adapted for it – the representation of contemporary and of recently past events – there was nothing, on the whole, but more or less inadequate attempts; in the epoch especially from Sulla to Caesar the not very important contributions, which the previous epoch had to show in this field – the labours of Antipater and Asellius – were barely even equalled.

The only work of note belonging to this field, which arose in the present epoch, was the history of the Social and Civil Wars by Lucius Cornelius Sisenna (praetor in 676 [78 BC]). Those who had read it testify that it far excelled in liveliness and readableness the old dry chronicles, but was written withal in a style thoroughly impure and even degenerating into puerility; as indeed the few remaining fragments exhibit a paltry painting of horrible details, and a number of words newly coined or derived from the language of conversation. When it is added that the author's model and, so to speak, the only Greek historian familiar to him was Clitarchus, the author of a biography of Alexander the Great oscillating between history and fiction in the manner of the semi-romance which bears the name of Curtius, we shall not hesitate to recognize in Sisenna's celebrated historical work, not a product of genuine historical criticism and art, but the first Roman essay in that hybrid mixture of history and romance so much a favourite with the Greeks, which desires to make the groundwork of facts life-like and interesting by means of fictitious details and thereby makes it insipid and untrue; and it will no longer excite surprise that we meet with the same Sisenna also as translator of Greek fashionable romances.

Annals of the City

That the prospect should be still more lamentable in the field of the general annals of the city and even of the world, was implied in the nature of the case. The increasing activity of antiquarian research induced the expectation that the current narrative would be rectified from documents and other trustworthy sources; but this hope was not fulfilled. The more and the deeper men investigated, the more clearly it became apparent what a task it was to write a critical history of Rome. The difficulties even, which opposed themselves to investigation and narration, were immense; but the most dangerous obstacles were not those of a literary kind. The conventional early history of Rome, as it had now been narrated and believed for at least ten generations, was most intimately mixed up with the civil life of the nation; and yet in any thorough and honest inquiry not only had details to be modified here and there, but the whole building had to be overturned as much as the Franconian primitive history of king Pharamund or the British of king Arthur.

An inquirer of conservative views, such as was Varro for instance, could have no wish to put his hand to such a work; and if a daring freethinker had undertaken it, an outcry would have been raised by all good citizens against this worst of all revolutionaries, who was preparing to deprive the constitutional party even of their past. Thus philological and antiquarian research deterred from the writing of history rather than conduced towards it. Varro and the more sagacious men in general evidently gave up the task of annals as hopeless; at the most they arranged, as did Titus Pomponius Atticus, the official and gentile lists in unpretending tabular shape – a work by which the synchronistic Graeco-Roman chronology was finally brought into the shape in which it was conventionally fixed for posterity. But the manufacture of city-chronicles of course did not suspend its activity; it continued to supply its contributions both in prose and verse to the great library written by ennui for ennui, while the makers of the books, in part already freedmen, did not trouble themselves at all about research properly so called. Such of these writings as are mentioned to us – not one of them is preserved – seem to have been not only of a wholly secondary character, but in great part even pervaded by interested falsification. It is true that the chronicle of Quintus Claudius Quadrigarius (about 676? [78 BC?]) was written in an old-fashioned but good style, and studied at least a commendable brevity in the representation of the fabulous period. Gaius Licinius Macer (d. as late praetor in 688 [66 BC]), father of the poet Calvus, and a zealous democrat, laid claim more than any other chronicler to documentary research and criticism, but his *libri lintei* and other matters peculiar to him are in the highest degree suspicious, and an interpolation of the whole annals in the interest of democratic tendencies – an interpolation of a very extensive kind, and which has passed over in part to the later annalists – is probably traceable to him.

Valerius Antias

Lastly, Valerius Antias excelled all his predecessors in prolixity as well as in puerile story-telling. The falsification of numbers was here systematically carried out down even to contemporary history, and the primitive history of Rome was elaborated once more from one form of insipidity to another; for instance the narrative of the way in which the wise Numa according to the instructions of the nymph Egeria caught the gods Faunus and Picus; with wine, and the beautiful conversation thereupon held by the same Numa with the god Jupiter, cannot be too urgently recommended to all worshippers of the so-called legendary history of Rome in order that, if possible, they may believe these things – of course, in substance. It would have been a marvel if the Greek novel-writers of this period had allowed such materials, made as if for their use, to escape them. In fact there were not wanting Greek literati, who worked up the Roman history into romances; such a composition, for instance, was the Five Books "Concerning Rome" of the Alexander Polyhistor already mentioned among the Greek literati living in Rome, a preposterous mixture of vapid historical tradition and trivial, principally erotic, fiction. He, it may be presumed, took the first steps towards filling up the five hundred years, which were wanting to bring the destruction of Troy and the origin of Rome into the chronological connection required by the fables on either side, with one of those lists of kings without achievements which are unhappily familiar to the Egyptian and Greek chroniclers; for, to all appearance, it was he that launched into the world the kings Aventinus and Tiberinus and the Alban gens of the Silvii, whom the following times accordingly did not neglect to furnish in detail with name, period of reigning, and, for the sake of greater definiteness, also a portrait.

Thus from various sides the historical romance of the Greeks finds its way into Roman historiography; and it is more than probable that not the least portion of what we are accustomed nowadays to call tradition of the Roman primitive times proceeds from sources of the stamp of Amadis of Gaul and the chivalrous romances of Fouque – an edifying consideration, at least for those who have a relish for the humour of history and who know how to appreciate the comical aspect of the piety still cherished in certain circles of the nineteenth century for king Numa.

Universal History – Nepos

A novelty in the Roman literature of this period is the appearance of universal history or, to speak more correctly, of Roman and Greek history conjoined, alongside of the native annals. Cornelius Nepos from Ticinum (c. 650–c. 725 [c. 104–c. 29 BC]) first supplied an universal chronicle (published before 700 [54 BC]) and a general collection of biographies – arranged according to certain categories – of Romans and Greeks distinguished in politics or literature or of men at any rate who exercised influence on the Roman or Greek history. These works are of a kindred nature with the universal histories which the Greeks had for a considerable time been composing; and these very Greek world-chronicles, such as that of Kastor son-in-law of the Galatian king Deiotarus, concluded in 698 [56 BC], now began to include in their range the Roman history which previously they had neglected. These works certainly attempted, just like Polybius, to substitute the history of the Mediterranean world for the more local one; but that which in Polybius was the result of a grand and clear conception and deep historical feeling was in these chronicles rather the product of the practical exigencies of school and self-instruction. These general chronicles, text-books for scholastic instruction or manuals for reference, and the whole literature therewith connected which subsequently became very copious in the Latin language also, can hardly be reckoned as belonging to artistic historical composition; and Nepos himself in particular was a pure compiler distinguished neither by spirit nor even merely by symmetrical plan.

The historiography of this period is certainly remarkable and in a high degree characteristic, but it is as far from pleasing as the age itself. The interpenetration of Greek and Latin literature is in no field so clearly apparent as in that of history; here the respective literatures become earliest equalized in matter and form, and the conception of Helleno-Italic history as an unity, in which Polybius was so far in advance of his age, was now learned even by Greek and Roman boys at school. But while the Mediterranean state had found a historian before it had become conscious of its own existence, now, when that consciousness had been attained, there did not arise either among the Greeks or among the Romans any man who was able to give to it adequate expression. "There is no such thing," says Cicero, "as Roman historical composition"; and, so far as we can judge, this is no more than the simple truth. The man of research turns away from writing history, the writer of history turns away from research; historical literature oscillates between the schoolbook and the romance. All the species of pure art – epos, drama, lyric poetry, history – are worthless in this worthless world; but in no species is the intellectual decay of the Ciceronian age reflected with so terrible a clearness as in its historiography.

Literature Subsidiary to History – Caesar's Report

The minor historical literature of this period displays on the other hand, amidst many insignificant and forgotten productions, one treatise of the first rank – the Memoirs of Caesar, or rather the Military Report of the democratic general to the people from whom he had received his commission. The finished section, and that which alone was published by the author himself, describing the Celtic campaigns down to 702 [52 BC], is evidently designed to justify as well as possible before the public the formally unconstitutional enterprise of Caesar in conquering a great country and constantly increasing his army for that object without instructions from the competent authority; it was written and given forth in 703 [51 BC], when the storm broke out against Caesar in Rome and he was summoned to dismiss his army and answer for his conduct. The author of this vindication writes, as he himself says, entirely as an officer and carefully avoids extending his military report to the hazardous departments of political organization and administration. His incidental and partisan treatise cast in the form of a military report is itself a piece of history like the bulletins of Napoleon, but it is not, and was not intended to be, a historical work in the true sense of the word; the objective form which the narrative assumes is that of the magistrate, not that of the historian. But in this modest character the work is masterly and finished, more than any other in all Roman literature. The narrative is always terse and never scanty, always simple and never careless, always of transparent vividness and never strained or affected. The language is completely pure from archaisms and from vulgarisms – the type of the modern *urbanitas*. In the Books concerning the Civil War we seem to feel that the author had desired to avoid war and could not avoid it, and perhaps also that in Caesar's soul, as in every other, the period of hope was a purer and fresher one than that of fulfilment; but over the treatise on the Gallic war there is diffused a bright serenity, a simple charm, which are no less unique in literature than Caesar is in history. ...

Rise of A Literature of Pleadings – Cicero

While the composition of orations thus declined from its former literary and political value in the same way as all branches of literature which were the natural growth of the national life, there began at the same time a singular, non-political, literature of pleadings. Hitherto the Romans had known nothing of the idea that the address of an advocate as such was destined not only for the judges and the parties, but also for the literary edification of contemporaries and posterity; no advocate had written down and published his pleadings, unless they were possibly at the same time political orations and in so far were fitted to be circulated as party writings, and this had not occurred very frequently. Even Quintus Hortensius (640–704 [114–50 BC]), the most celebrated Roman advocate in the first years of this period, published but few speeches and these apparently only such as were wholly or half political. It was his successor in the leadership of the Roman bar, Marcus Tullius Cicero (648–711 [106–43 BC]) who was from the outset quite as much author as forensic orator; he published his pleadings regularly, even when they were not at all or but remotely connected with politics. This was a token, not of progress, but of an unnatural and degenerate state of things. Even in Athens the appearance of non-political pleadings among the forms of literature was a sign of debility; and it was doubly so in Rome, which did not, like Athens, by a sort of necessity produce this malformation from the exaggerated pursuit of rhetoric, but borrowed it from abroad arbitrarily and in antagonism to the better traditions of the nation. Yet this new species of literature came rapidly into vogue, partly because it had various points of contact and coincidence with the earlier authorship of political orations, partly because the unpoetic, dogmatical, rhetorizing temperament of the Romans offered a favourable soil for the new seed, as indeed at the present day the speeches of advocates and even a sort of literature of law-proceedings are of some importance in Italy.

His Character

Thus oratorical authorship emancipated from politics was naturalized in the Roman literary world by Cicero. We have already had occasion several times to mention this many-sided man. As a statesman without insight, idea, or purpose, he figured successively as democrat, as aristocrat, and as a tool of the monarchs, and was never more than a short-sighted egotist. Where he exhibited the semblance of action, the questions to which his action applied had, as a rule, just reached their solution; thus he came forward in the trial of Verres against the senatorial courts when they were already set aside; thus he was silent at the discussion on the Gabinian, and acted as a champion of the Manilian law; thus he thundered against Catilina when his departure was already settled, and so forth.

He was valiant in opposition to sham attacks, and he knocked down many walls of pasteboard with a loud din; no serious matter was ever, either in good or evil, decided by him, and the execution of the Catilinarians in particular was far more due to his acquiescence than to his instigation. In a literary point of view we have already noticed that he was the creator of the modern Latin prose; his importance rests on his mastery of style, and it is only as a stylist that he shows confidence in himself.

In the character of an author, on the other hand, he stands quite as low as in that of a statesman. He essayed the most varied tasks, sang the great deeds of Marius and his own petty achievements in endless hexameters, beat Demosthenes off the field with his speeches, and Plato with his philosophic dialogues; and time alone was wanting for him to vanquish also Thucydides. He was in fact so thoroughly a dabbler, that it was pretty much a matter of indifference to what work he applied his hand.

By nature a journalist in the worst sense of that term – abounding, as he himself says, in words, poor beyond all conception in ideas – there was no department in which he could not with the help of a few books have rapidly got up by translation or compilation a readable essay. His correspondence mirrors most faithfully his character. People are in the habit of calling it interesting and clever; and it is so, as long as it reflects the urban or villa life of the world of quality; but where the writer is thrown on his own resources, as in exile, in Cilicia, and after the battle of Pharsalus, it is stale and empty as was ever the soul of a feuilletonist banished from his familiar circles. It is scarcely needful to add that such a statesman and such a *litterateur* could not, as a man, exhibit aught else than a thinly varnished superficiality and heart-lessness.

Must we still describe the orator? The great author is also a great man; and in the great orator more especially conviction or passion flows forth with a clearer and more impetuous stream from the depths of the breast than in the scantily-gifted many who merely count and are nothing. Cicero had no conviction and no passion; he was nothing but an advocate, and not a good one. He understood how to set forth his narrative of the case with piquancy of anecdote, to excite, if not the feeling, at any rate the sentimentality of his hearers, and to enliven the dry business of legal pleading by cleverness or witticisms mostly of a personal sort; his better orations, though they are far from coming up to the free gracefulness and the sure point of the most excellent compositions of this sort, for instance the Memoirs of Beaumarchais, yet form easy and agreeable reading. But while the very advantages just indicated will appear to the serious judge as advantages of very dubious value, the absolute want of political discernment in the orations on constitutional questions and of juristic deduction in the forensic addresses, the egotism forgetful of its duty and constantly losing sight of the cause while thinking of the advocate, the dreadful barrenness of thought in the Ciceronian orations must revolt every reader of feeling and judgment.

Ciceronianism

If there is anything wonderful in the case, it is in truth not the orations, but the admiration which they excited. As to Cicero every unbiassed person will soon make up his mind: Ciceronianism is a problem, which in fact cannot be properly solved, but can only be resolved into that greater mystery of human nature – language and the effect of language on the mind. Inasmuch as the noble Latin language, just before it perished as a national idiom, was once more as it were comprehensively grasped by that dexterous stylist and deposited in his copious writings, something of the power which language exercises, and of the piety which it awakens, was transferred to the unworthy vessel. The Romans possessed no great Latin prosewriter; for Caesar was, like Napoleon, only incidentally an author. Was it to be wondered at that, in the absence of such an one, they should at least honour the genius of the language in the great stylist? And that, like Cicero himself, Cicero's readers also should accustom themselves to ask not what, but how he had written? Custom and the schoolmaster then completed what the power of language had begun.

Opposition to Ciceronianism – Calvus and His Associates

Cicero's contemporaries however were, as may readily be conceived, far less involved in this strange idolatry than many of their successors. The Ciceronian manner ruled no doubt throughout a generation the Roman advocate-world, just as the far worse manner of Hortensius had done; but the most considerable men, such as Caesar, kept themselves always aloof from it, and among the younger generation there arose in all men of fresh and living talent the most decided opposition to that hybrid and feeble rhetoric. They found Cicero's language deficient in precision and chasteness, his jests deficient in liveliness, his arrangement deficient in clearness and articulate division, and above all his whole eloquence wanting in the fire which makes the orator. ... The time allotted to them was but too brief. The new monarchy began by making war on freedom of speech, and soon wholly suppressed the political oration. Thenceforth the subordinate species of the pure advocate-pleading was doubtless still retained in literature; but the higher art and literature of oratory, which thoroughly depend on political excitement, perished with the latter of necessity and for ever. ...

Conclusion

We have reached the end of the Roman republic. We have seen it rule for five hundred years in Italy and in the countries on the Mediterranean; we have seen it brought to ruin in politics and morals, religion and literature, not through outward violence but through inward decay, and thereby making room for the new monarchy of Caesar. There was in the world, as Caesar found it, much of the noble heritage of past centuries and an infinite abundance of pomp and glory, but little spirit, still less taste, and least of all true delight in life. It was indeed an old world; and even the richly-gifted patriotism of Caesar could not make it young again. The dawn does not return till after the night has fully set in and run its course. But yet with him there came to the sorely harassed peoples on the Mediterranean a tolerable evening after the sultry noon; and when at length after a long historical night the new day dawned once more for the peoples, and fresh nations in free self-movement commenced their race towards new and higher goals, there were found among them not a few, in which the seed sown by Caesar had sprung up, and which owed, as they still owe, to him their national individuality.

So now, we turn to our text, translated and expanded with editorial inclusions and footnotes as described above.

Acknowledgements

Thanks go to Michael Franzl for translating the German text, Harrison Koehli and Irini Gregoriou for assistance with Latin and Greek translations, and Jason Martin for a critical reading of the text and cover design.

Antias and Caesar

After Mommsen gave so bleak an insight into Roman historiography – as he remarks at the end of his work – and gave us inducement to undertake the present work, we now face a result that makes us even more suspicious regarding the post-Caesarian transmissions. It is likely that others will be able to find more hidden clues of a similar nature in Livy and Dionysius than the one herein presented.

According to orally transmitted tradition, it is known that Brutus forced all Romans to never again allow another king to rule over Rome. This is a process that is unique in all of Roman history. One may be tempted to compare the *"leges sacratae"*[10] in parallel with the contract regarding the tribunes that was made between the citizens and the plebs following the first secession. But, as the term says, it was a contract, a regulation, that was put under the protection of the gods by a vow,[11] where a *lex* **precedes** the vow. That is, the law came first and the vow to uphold the law came after. In Roman history we know of several purely legal condemnations of exceptional magistrates,[12] but none of them can be compared with the event in question here. The following authors will be examined in an effort to shed light on this problem: Livy,[13] Dionysius of Halicarnassus,[14] Cicero's *De Re Publica*, Plutarch's *Publicola*, Valerius Maximus,[15] Cassius

---

[10] 494 BC: law after first secession of the plebeians that either affirmed the sacrosanctity of the tribunes or established the plebeians as a sworn confederacy against patricians

[11] Schwegler, *Römische Geschichte*, 2.250 sq.

[12] We will examine the *lex Valeria Publicolae* later on, which belongs to this category.

[13] Titus Livius Patavinus (59 BC–AD 17) – known as Livy in English – was a Roman historian who wrote a monumental history of Rome and the Roman people, *Ab Urbe Condita Libri*, "Books from the Foundation of the City", covering the period from the earliest legends of Rome well before the traditional foundation in 753 BC through the reign of Augustus in Livy's own time. He was on familiar terms with the Julio-Claudian family, advising Augustus's grandnephew, the future emperor Claudius, as a young man. [Ed.]

[14] Dionysius of Halicarnassus, c. 60–after 7 BC, was a Greek historian and teacher of rhetoric, who flourished during the reign of Caesar Augustus. [Ed.]

[15] Valerius Maximus was a Latin writer and author of a collection of historical anecdotes.

Dio,[16] Appian.[17] Livy mentions this vow twice, firstly as follows:

> *Omnium primum avidum novae libertatis populum, ne postmodum flecti precibus ant donis regiis posset, iure iurando adegit, neminem Romae passuros regnare.*[18]

To begin with, when the people were still jealous of their new freedom, he [Brutus] obliged them to swear an oath that they would suffer no man to be king in Rome, lest they might later be turned from their purpose by the entreaties of the gifts of princes.

Secondly, because the young Republic seemed to be endangered by the fact that one of the first two consuls carried the name Tarquinius, Brutus tried to persuade him to leave Rome and called the vow into mind:

> *Plebem ad contionem vocat. Ibi omnium primum ius iurandum populi recitat: neminem regnare passuros nec esse Romae, unde periculum libertati foret.*[19]

Brutus summoned the people to an assembly. There he first of all recited the oath which the people had taken, that they would suffer no king in Rome, nor any man who might be dangerous to liberty.

He wrote during the reign of Tiberius (AD 14–37). Nothing is known of his life except that his family was poor and undistinguished, and that he owed everything to Sextus Pompeius (consul AD 14), proconsul of Asia, whom he accompanied to the East in 27. Pompeius was the center of a literary circle to which Ovid belonged; he was also an intimate friend of the most literary prince of the imperial family, Germanicus. The author's chief sources are Cicero, Livy, Sallust, and Pompeius Trogus, especially the first two. Valerius's treatment of his material is careless and unintelligent in the extreme. [Ed.]

[16] Lucius (or Claudius) Cassius Dio (alleged to have the cognomen Cocceianus), c. AD 155–235, known in English as Cassius Dio, Dio Cassius, or Dio, was a Roman consul and noted historian who wrote in Greek. Dio published a history of Rome in 80 volumes, beginning with the legendary arrival of Aeneas in Italy; the volumes then documented the subsequent founding of Rome (753 BC), the formation of the Republic (509 BC), and the creation of the Empire (31 BC), up until AD 229. The entire period covered by Dio's work is approximately 1,400 years. Of the 80 books, written over 22 years, many survive into the modern age, intact, or as fragments, providing modern scholars with a detailed perspective on Roman history. [Ed.]

[17] Appian of Alexandria (c. AD 95–c. 165) was a Roman historian of Greek ethnicity who flourished during the reigns of Emperors of Rome Trajan, Hadrian, and Antoninus Pius. [Ed.]

[18] Livy, *History of Rome*, 2.1.9.

[19] Ibid., 2.2.4.

On the second occasion we find a small, insignificant extension where Brutus adds corroboratively:

id summa ope esse tuendum neque ullam rem, quae eo pertineat, contemnendam

This oath they must uphold, he said, with all their might, nor make light of anything which bore upon it.

Because both quotes are so similar, it hardly can be doubted that in both cases Livy used the same source. Dionysius is more explicit:

... καὶ μετὰ τοῦτο ... ὅρκια τεμόντες, αὐτοί τε πρῶτοι στάντες ἐπὶ τῶν τομίων ὤμοσαν, μὴ κατάξειν ἀπὸ τῆς φυγῆς βασιλέα Ταρκύνιον, μήτε τοὺς παῖδας αὐτοῦ, μήτε τοὺς ἐξ ἐκείνων γενησομένους, βασιλέα δὲ τῆς Ῥωμαίων πόλεως μηκέτι καταστήσειν μηδένα, μηδὲ τοῖς καθιστάναι βουλομένοις ἐπιτρέψειν. Ταῦτα μὲν περὶ ἑαυτῶν τε καὶ τῶν τέκνων καὶ τοῦ μεθ᾽ἑαυτοὺς γένους ὤμοσαν.

Lucius Junius Brutus and Lucius Tarquinius Collatinus were the first consuls invested with the royal power ... [They] called an assembly of the people a few days after the expulsion of the tyrant, and having spoken at length upon the advantages of harmony, again caused them to pass another vote confirming everything which those in the city had previously voted when condemning the Tarquinii to perpetual banishment. After this they performed rites of purification for the city and entered into a solemn covenant ... and they themselves ... first swore, and then prevailed upon the rest of the citizens likewise to swear, that they would never restore from exile King Tarquinius or his sons or their posterity, and that they would never again make anyone king of Rome or permit others who wished it to do so; and this oath they took not only for themselves but also for their children and their posterity.[20]

Later, as a delegation of Tarquinius came and asked for his return, Brutus answered them that this was impossible:

... ἐπῆκται γὰρ ἤδη ψῆφος ἀίδιον κατ᾽ αὐτῶν ὁρίζουσα φυγὴν καὶ θεοὺς ὀμομώκαμεν ἅπαντες, μητ᾽ αὐτοὶ κατάξειν τοὺς τυράννους μηδὲ τοῖς κατάγουσιν ἐπιτρέπειν

---

[20]Dionysius, *Roman Antiquities*, 5.1.

For a vote has already been passed condemning them to perpetual banishment, and we have all sworn by the gods neither to restore the tyrants ourselves nor to permit others to restore them.[21]

Contrary to Livy, the vow is different in such a way that first, the entire family of Tarquinius is banned, and only after that, the vow is extended into all of eternity. The obvious reason why this addition is missing from the second place is that a direct answer was only given to the direct request of the delegation.

Appian briefly connects the vow to Caesar's murderers:

> ἐπί τε τὴν πάτριον πολιτείαν παρεκάλουν καὶ Βρούτου τοῦ πάλαι καὶ τῶν τότε σφίσιν ὠμοσμένων ἐπὶ τοῖς πάλαι βασιλεῦσιν ἀνεμίμνησκον
>
> ... and recall the memory of the elder Brutus and of those who took the oath together against the ancient kings.[22]

Finally, Plutarch:

> Ἐπεὶ δὲ καὶ πρὸς ἑτέρους τινὰς ὑποψίαν ἔχων ὁ Βροῦτος ἐβούλετο διὰ σφαγίων ὁρκῶσαι τὴν βονλὴν καὶ προεῖπεν ἡμέραν, καταβὰς μάλα σφαίδρος εἰς ἀγορὰν ὁ Οὐαλλέριος, καὶ πρῶτος ὁμόσας μηδὲν ἐνδώσειν μηδ᾽ ὑφήσεσθαι Ταρκυνίοις, ἀλλὰ πολεμήσειν κατὰ κράτος ὑπὲρ τῆς ἐλευθερίας.
>
> But when Brutus, who had his suspicions of certain others also, desired the senators to take a sacrificial oath, and set a day for the ceremony, Valerius went down into the forum, and was the first to take oath that he would make no submission or concession to the Tarquinii, but would fight with all his might in defense of freedom.[23]

I want to examine the different renderings – by different sources – of this important event a little more closely. The most detailed version of the vow, and most rich in substance, is reported by Dionysius. He reports a natural development within a believable context. First, he brings up the law to ban the Tarquinii forever and to punish with death him who dares to bring them back. Then, the vow is extended in such a way that everyone

---

[21] Dionysius, *Roman Antiquities*, 5.5.
[22] Appian, *Civil Wars*, 17.119.
[23] Plutarch, *Life of Publicola*, 2.

has to promise to himself and to his children that they never will allow another king to rule over Rome again, and to not allow anyone to reinstate kingship. For some strange reason, however, Livy skips over this special case entirely and mentions rather suddenly, and without the progression [Ed.: of voting, purification, etc.], the outlawing of the kingship by oath of all the people. Opposed to that is Appian where we only find the vow that "went against the ancient kings" (τότε... ἐπὶ τοῖς πάλαι) mentioned in passing. Most believable is the story of Plutarch who reports that Brutus – fearing a conspiracy – had the Senate (not the entire populace) swear to never let the Tarquinii return. We can find this general application of the vow to **all the people** only in Livy and Dionysius. I will come back to the differences of the individual reports further on.

At this point we have exhausted our sources, which are indeed shallow for such an important event. Mommsen wondered[24] about the strange monosyllabic way of recounting this important tradition, but he reasoned that it was due to the circumstances of the time of Augustus, where talk about the vow was taboo, because, **if** it had been recorded historically, the murder of Caesar would have been justified juristically or rather quasi-juristically. But we probably have to negate this cause for the following reasons. First of all, Dionysius, who sets himself apart from the others by his detailed report, was a Caesarian himself. With such a consideration of Augustus – the relative of the murdered Caesar – would the Valerian law[25] – *de sacreando cum bonis capite eius qui regni occupandi consilia inisset* [Ed.: the confiscation and/or destruction of the possessions and property of any conspirator],[26] and its apparent[27] consequences, such as

---

[24] Mommsen, *Römisches Staatsrecht*, II^1, p. 15.

[25] Enacted by Publius Valerius Publicola in 509 BC. It provided for appeal to the people composed of senators, patricians, and plebeians, in capital cases. The original Valerian law was also claimed to have made it legal to kill any citizen who was plotting to seize a tyranny, which is the specific reference here. The Valerian law was apparently not kept on the books throughout the alleged five hundred years of the Roman Republic. Livy states that the Valerian law was enacted again, for the third time, in 299 BC. Livy notes that in all three cases the law was enacted by a member of the Valerius family. Furthermore, Livy notes that, should a magistrate disregard the Valerian law, his only reproof was that his act be deemed unlawful and wicked. This implies that the Valerian law was not so very effective in defending the plebs. [Ed.]

[26] Livy, *History of Rome*, 2.8.2.

[27] You will find the reason why I used the word "apparent" in my later investigation

occurred with the murders of Spurius Maelius,[28] Spurius Cassius,[29] Marcus Manlius[30] – receive such extensive attention from Livy and Dionysius?

What catches our attention here mostly is not only the shortness of the account, but the complete absence of the mention of a vow in Cicero. This fact alone is very strange, but weighs even heavier when we consider that Cicero often discussed the elimination of the kingship but never mentioned any vow. To really feel the strangeness of this silence we must take a closer look at all the individual literary items. Here, I particularly note the report about the eviction of Tarquinius in *De Re Publica* 2.46.

---

into the *lex Valeria Publicolae.*

[28] Spurius Maelius (d. 439 BC), a wealthy Roman plebeian, who during a severe famine bought up a large amount of wheat and sold it at a low price to the people. Lucius Minucius Augurinus, the patrician *praefectus annonae* (president of the market), thereupon accused him of courting popularity with a view to making himself king. He was slain by Gaius Servilius Ahala; his house was razed to the ground, his wheat distributed amongst the people, and his property confiscated. Cicero calls Ahala's deed a glorious one, but, whether Maelius entertained any ambitious projects or not, his summary execution was an act of murder, since by the Valerio-Horatian laws the dictator was bound to allow the right of appeal. [Ed.]

[29] Spurius Cassius Viscellinus or Vecellinus (d. 485 BC) was one of the most distinguished men of the early Roman Republic. He was three times consul, and celebrated two triumphs. He was the first *magister equitum*, and the author of the first agrarian law. The year following his last consulship, he was accused of aiming at regal power. He was tried and sentenced to death by his fellow patricians, who regarded him a traitor for siding with the plebeians. Cassius was scourged and beheaded; his house razed to the ground, and the spot where it stood, in front of the temple of Tellus, was left waste. [Ed.]

[30] Marcus Manlius Capitolinus (d. 384 BC) was consul of the Roman Republic in 392 BC. After the sack of Rome left the plebeians in pitiful condition, they were forced to borrow large sums of money from the patricians and once again became the poor debtor class of Rome. Manlius, the hero of Rome, fought for them. Seeing a centurion led to prison for debt, he freed him with his own money and even sold his estate to relieve other poor debtors, while he accused the Senate of embezzling public money. He was charged with aspiring to kingly power and condemned by the *comitia*, but not until the assembly had adjourned to a place outside the walls, where they could no longer see the Capitol which he had saved. The Senate condemned him to death in 385 BC, and he was thrown from the Tarpeian Rock one year later. His house on the Capitoline Hill was razed, and the Senate decreed that no patrician should live there henceforth. The Manlii themselves resolved that no patrician Manlius should bear the name of Marcus. According to Mommsen, the story of the saving of the Capitol was a later invention to justify his cognomen, which may be better explained by his domicile. [Ed.]

> L. Brutus depulit a civibus suis iniustum illud durae servitutis iugum. qui cum privatus esset, totam rem publicam sustinuit primusque in hac civitate docuit in conservanda libertate esse privatum neminem. quo auctore et principe concitata civitas et hac recenti querella Lucretiaa patris ac propinquorum et recordatione superbiae Tarquinii multarumque iniuriarum et ipsius et filiorum, exsulem et regem ipsum et liberos eius et gentem Tarquiniorum esse iussit.

Lucius Brutus, a man pre-eminent for wisdom and bravery, freed his fellow-citizens from the unjust yoke of cruel servitude. And though Brutus was only a private citizen, he sustained the whole burden of the government, and was the first in our state to demonstrate that no one is a mere private citizen when the liberty of his fellows needs protection. On his initiative and under his leadership, the people, aroused not only by the bitter complaints still fresh in their memories of Lucretia's father and kinsmen, but also by their own recollection of the pride of Tarquinius and the many acts of injustice committed by him and his sons, banished the king himself, his children, and the whole race of the Tarquinii.

In paragraph 46 the handwritten account is complete and in beautiful context. The report is only about the expulsion of the Tarquinii. In 1.62 and 2.52 he speaks about the hatred of the public against the kingship, but does not explain this with a vow. Then, one should pay attention to *Brutus* 53:

> [Brutus] qui potentissimum regem, clarissimi regis filium expulerit, civitatem perpetuo dominatu liberatam magistratibus annuis, ligibus, iudiciisque devinxerit, qui conlegae suo imperium abrogaverit, ut e civitate regalis nominis memoriam tolleret ...

Who dethroned and banished a powerful monarch [Tarquinius], the son of an illustrious sovereign? Who settled the state, which he had rescued from arbitrary power, by the appointment of an annual magistracy, a regular system of laws, and a free and open course of justice? And who abrogated the authority of his colleague [Lucius Tarquinius Collatinus], that he might rid the city of the smallest vestige of the regal name?

Here, Cicero would never have ignored a vow if it had been mentioned in his sources, especially because he lists by which means Brutus had consolidated the Republic.[31]

But the greatest curiosity is: Why would he have wanted to not mention a such weighty argument – to incite against the threatening kingship of Caesar – in his letters to Brutus and Atticus? We cannot find a compelling reason for an intentional silence or for carelessness of Cicero. Hence, he obviously **did not know** about a vow, and was not silent because of historical ignorance, but because such a report was not available.

We can draw another important conclusion from this. For the *De Re Publica*, Cicero has drawn from the most important historians who are regarded as the main authorities on Roman history available during his time. He took his theoretical perspectives from Plato, Aristotle, and Theophrastus, while for the positive parts he drew from Polybius[32] and Ennius,[33] whose names he mentions several times. Hence, they didn't mention anything about a vow either – at least it is likely that they didn't – and this fact essentially proves that Cicero's historical credibility is not too far-fetched. I also want to mention the *auctor ad Herrenium*,[34] which

---

[31] It would require too much space to quote other sources directly. Notable sources are: *De Officiis* 3.40; *Philippica* 3.8; 2.87; *De Amicitia* 28; *De Re Publica* 1.62 and 64; *ad Atticum* 14.3.2; and others.

[32] Cicero, *De Re Publica*, 1.34; 2.27; 4.3.

[33] Cicero, *De Re Publica*, 1.3, 25, 30, and 62; 3.6; 5.1; Cicero, *Fragments*, inc. 9, 10.

[34] The current scholarly opinion is that this was written by Quintus Cornificius. Internal indications point to the date of compositions as 86–82 BC, the period of Marian domination in Rome. The unknown author, as may be inferred from the treatise itself, did not write to make money, but to oblige his relative and friend Herennius, for whose instruction he promises to supply other works on grammar, military matters, and political administration. He expresses his contempt for the ordinary school rhetorician, the hair-splitting dialecticians and their sense of inability to speak, since they dare not even pronounce their own name for fear of expressing themselves ambiguously. Finally, he admits that rhetoric is not the highest accomplishment and that philosophy is far more deserving of attention. Politically, it is evident that he was a staunch supporter of the popular party. The question of the relation of Cicero's *De Inventione* to the *Rhetorica* has been much discussed. Three views were held: that the Auctor copied from Cicero; that they were independent of each other, parallelisms being due to their having been taught by the same rhetorician at Rome; and that Cicero made extracts from the Rhetorica, as well as from other authorities, in his usual eclectic fashion. One of the 19th century editors, Friedrich Marx, puts forward the theory that Cicero and the Auctor have not produced original works, but have merely given the substance of two technai (both emanating from the Rhodian school); that neither used them directly, but reproduced the revised version of the rhetoricians whose school they attended, the introductions alone being their

also silently ignores this event:³⁵

> quodsi nunc Lucius ille Brutus reviviscat et hic ante pedes vestros adsit, is non hac utatur oratione: "ego reges eieci, vos tyrannos introducitis; ego libertatem, quae non erat, peperi, vos partam servare non voltis; ego capitis mei periculo patriam liberavi, vos liberi sine periculo esse non curatis?
>
> Again: "But if that great Lucius Brutus should now come to life again and appear here before you, would he not use this language? 'I banished kings; you bring in tyrants. I created liberty, which did not exist; what I created you do not wish to preserve. I, at peril of my life, freed the fatherland; you, even without peril, do not care to be free.'"³⁶

It would have been unforgivable for a writer to omit such a vow in this context, because he could have used it in a beautiful way to bolster his literary eloquence. This work originates in the Sullan time between 86 and 82. At this time, this vow had not yet been reported [Ed.: was neither a tradition nor a matter of common knowledge]. For the mentioned reasons it is clear that this entire issue must have been created at a later time. We are dealing with a falsification that shows a particular tendency.

Mommsen has proven in an essay about the "Scipionenprozesse" ("The legal actions concerning Scipio")³⁷ that Caesar was attacked under the mask of Scipio.³⁸ I will investigate this essay at a later point. Our current issue is very similar to that one, but it is more far-reaching than the one discovered by Mommsen, even if it has not been interwoven with history in such an elaborate way.

Let me also draw your attention to an inner contradiction in Livy. If the vow had exactly been what has been reported about it – with its profound obligation – then the transfer of power to the first magistrates of Rome could have been an offense, because the unlimited authority of the state

---

own work; and that the lectures on which the Ciceronian treatise was based were delivered before the lectures attended by the Auctor. [Ed.]

³⁵Marx, *Rhetorica ad Herennium*, 4.66.
³⁶Cicero, *Rhetorica ad Herennium*.
³⁷Mommsen, "Die Scipionenprozesse".
³⁸Mommsen, *Römische Forschungen*, II, p. 417.

was transferred from the king to the consuls.[39] Later, Livy used phrases like *"consulare imperium nomine tantum minus invidiosum, re ipsa prope atrocius quam regium esse"* [the authority of the consuls, as a thing excessive and intolerable in a free state][40] or *"regiae maiestatis imperium"* [a power regal in its majesty][41] and *"consules, regia potestas"* [consuls with the power of kings].[42] That surely conflicted with the obligation that was accepted: *"nec esse Romae, unde libertati periculum foret"* [never to be at Rome because it was a danger to liberty] and even more with the saying of Brutus: *"neque ullam rem, quae eo pertineat, [esse] contemnandam"* [anything resembling it [kingly power] is to be condemned]. But I want to return to the basic tendency of the whole falsification and point out a detail in Caesar's life that provided the impetus for it.

Due to the apparently acute concern of the Senate to secure the approval of the all-powerful dictator, the Senate demonstrated an outsized concern for Caesar's life and had made the decision to send out a number of knights and senators to protect him permanently.[43] In addition, all senators were required to swear a vow to protect the dictator's life and honour [Ed.: with their own].[44] After that, Caesar dismissed his personal bodyguard[45] but did not accept the Senate's protection [Ed.: in replacement]. By this he demonstrated great trust that he was **protected by the vow** of the Senate. This assumed duty was holy, and the murderers of Caesar – who consisted of knights and senators – were guilty of breaking this vow; even more because the murder was committed during a Senate meeting. That provided the Caesarians and avengers of the murdered dictator with a handle with which to direct the hatred of the populace against these men, and they did so skillfully. Let us compare Suetonius first:

Laudationis loco consul Antonius per praeconem pronuntiavit senatus

---

[39] Napoleon, *Histoire de Jules César*, I, p. 24; "All the rights of the kings and all their insignia were possessed by the earliest consuls ..." Livy, *History of Rome*, 2.1.

[40] Livy, *History of Rome*, 3.4.

[41] Ibid., 4.2.

[42] Livy, *History of Rome*, 8.32; Dionysius, *Roman Antiquities*, 7.35; Cicero, *De Re Publica*, 2.32 and 56; Cicero, *De Legibus*, 3.38. Maximus, *Factorum et Dictorum Memorabilium*, 4.1.1.

[43] Drumann, *Geschichte Roms*, III, p. 348; Lange, *Römische Altertümer*, III, p. 476.

[44] Suetonius, *Ceasar*, 84; 86; Appian, *Civil Wars*, 2.124 and 145; Dio, *Roman History*, 44.6.1; 7.4.

[45] Appian, *Civil Wars*, 2.109; Suetonius, *Ceasar*, 86; Dio, *Roman History*, 44.7.4.

consultum, quo omnia simul ei divina atque humana decreverat, item ius iurandum, quo se cuncti pro salute unius astrinxerant ...

Instead of a eulogy the consul Antonius caused a herald to recite the decree of the Senate in which it had voted Caesar all divine and human honours at once, and likewise the oath with which they had all pledged themselves to watch over his personal safety; to which he added a very few words of his own.[46]

... confisum eum [Caesarem] novissimo illo senatus consulto ac iure iurando etiam custodias Hispanorum cum gladiis adinspectantium se removisse.

... it was because [Caesar] had full trust in the last decree of the senators and their oath that he dismissed even the armed bodyguard of Spanish soldiers that formerly attended him.[47]

Appian points this out even clearer. There, Lepidus is prompted to avenge Caesar; others shout that he ought to give back peace to the city. He answered them:

... βουλόμεθα . ἀλλὰ ποίαν λέγετε εἰρήνην; ἢ ποίοις ὅρκοις ἀσφαλὴς ἔσται; τοὺς μὲν γὰρ πατρίους πάντας ὠμόσαμεν Καίσαρι καὶ κατεπατήσαμεν, οἱ τῶν ὀμωμοκότων ἄριστοι εἶναι λεγόμενοι.

We all swore the national oaths to Caesar and we have trampled on them – we who are considered the most distinguished of the oath-takers.[48]

In his own words, Antonius emphasizes this point most clearly and emphasizes it even more than the thankfulness that the populace had to have extended to its benefactor. Regarding the creation of proscription-lists, he at first uses this point to argue against the benevolence of Octavian because utter ruthlessness had to be applied:

ἕνεκα δὲ τοῦ μύσους καὶ ὧν Καίσαρι πάντες ὠμόσαμεν, φύλακες αὐτῷ τοῦ σώματος ἢ τιμωροὶ παθόντι τι ἔσεσθαι, εὔορκον ἦν τὸ ἄγος ἐξελαύνειν, καὶ μετ' ὀλιγωτέρων καθαρῶν βιοῦν μᾶλλον ἢ πάντας ἐνόχους ὄντας ταῖς ἀραῖς.

---

[46] Suetonius, *Ceasar*, 84.
[47] Ibid., 86.
[48] Appian, *Civil Wars*, 2.131.

We shall do nothing from private enmity, yet in consequence of the oaths we have all sworn to Caesar, that we would either protect his person or avenge his death, a solemn regard for our oath requires us to drive out the guilty and to live with a smaller number of innocent men rather than that all should be liable to the divine curse.[49]

While calling the populace for revenge, he brings the vow back to mind:

καὶ αὖθις ἀνεγίγνωσκε τοὺς ὅρκους, ἦ μὴν φυλάξειν Καίσαρα καὶ τὸ Καίσαρος σῶμα παντὶ σθένει πάντας, ἢ εἴ τις ἐπιβουλεύσειεν, ἐξώλεις εἶναι τοὺς οὐκ ἀμύναντας αὐτῷ. ἐφ' ὅτῳ δὴ μάλιστα τὴν φωνὴν ἐπιτείνας, καὶ τὴν χεῖρα ἐς τὸ Καπιτώλιον ἀνασχών· ἐγὼ μέν εἶπεν, ὦ Ζεῦ πάτριε καὶ θεοί, ἕτοιμος ἀμύνειν ὡς ὤμοσα καὶ ἠρασάμην. ἐπεὶ δὲ τοῖς ὁμοτίμοις δοκεῖ συνοίσειν τὰ ἐγνωσμένα, συνενεγκεῖν εὔχομαι.

Antonius resumed his reading and recited the oaths by which all were pledged to guard Caesar and Caesar's body with all their strength, and all were devoted to perdition who should not avenge him against any conspiracy. Here, lifting up his voice and extending his hand toward the Capitol, he exclaimed, "Jupiter, guardian of this city, and ye other gods, I stand ready to avenge him as I have sworn and vowed, but since those who are of equal rank with me have considered the decree of amnesty beneficial, I pray that it may prove to be so.[50]

Even though Antonius probably wasn't a man who, due to the vow, felt obliged to be an avenger, he nevertheless probably was skillful enough to play this vow against his enemies by pointing it out regularly, to cloak all his doings in an aura of holiness. Such means worked in Rome, and even though the religious perspectives weren't as strict as those of their ancestors, religious feelings still were very much alive so that one could count on them. The Optimates undoubtedly knew this and took advantage of it by using the gods as their justification.

Obviously, Antonius now had the law on his side, because he presented the revenge for Caesar as a religious necessity to the senators and the populace. But how did the murderers and the Republicans, who were happy about the deed, respond to the grave accusation that was played against them? That they had broken their promise [Ed.: of protecting

---

[49] Appian, *Civil Wars*, 2.124.
[50] Ibid., 2.145.

Caesar] was clearly seen by everyone and could not be hidden. The only defense for them, the only solution, was to have something that would have rendered their promise invalid; and that only could have been an earlier vow to which they had been bound, one that deprived the later vow of legal force.

The deed of Servilius Ahala could serve as a precedent for the murder of tyrants, of which Brutus was reminded because of his kinship with him. But this precedent and all other murders of tyrants could not serve as an excuse against the accusation of making a false oath [Ed.: i.e., the vow to protect Caesar]. Nothing could be found in their history that could excuse or ameliorate this breaking of the oath to protect Caesar; and so they resolved to a ruthlessly applied method in Roman history: a falsification.

What would have been more natural than to attempt a falsification of the history about the expulsion of kings, and to connect it to Brutus, who was seen as the progenitor of the murder of Caesar, a shining example from which the final expulsion of kings dated? He therefore became the originator of the invented vow that denied the kingship and that spoke of outlawing it everywhere and throughout time. If the murderers succeeded in giving credibility to such a story, then they would have attained a double goal: they would have freed themselves from the [Ed.: allegation of] making a false oath, plus, their deed would appear in a shining light; they would have gotten rid of a man who daily sneered at the Republican traditions and who did not hesitate to accept the crown of a king.

The murderers appear to have achieved their goal: whenever we read exuberant reports about the murder of a tyrant, the names of the assassins of Caesar usually appear first and foremost as [Ed.: precedental role models]. It would go too far to elaborate on the consequences of this discovery, but I at least would like to mention that the whole character of the conspiracy against Caesar now appears in a completely different light, and that the idealized glamor of the assassins – that they were freedom fighters – has been stripped away.

Was there only one source from which authors, who reported about the [Ed.: invented] vow, derived their tale? We can assume that it is most certain. The small differences in the accounts do not contradict this assumption because the differences do not conflict. The source was probably closest to the story as it is found in Dionysius, and nothing would have been more natural than to just add a little to the expulsion of the Tarquinii, such as a holy vow respecting the prohibition of the kingship for all of eternity. The fact that Livy only emphasized the part about all eternity was probably due to the fact that to him – an enthusiastic fan of the Republic – this specific case was not too important; and that would be why he unconsciously played into the original intention of the falsifier, for whom this element must have been most important. In Plutarch the most obvious tendency is to justify the murderers – who were members of the Senate – thanks to the vow, because, according to him, only senators made the vow. If he differs in this point from others, this does not deny the possibility of a single source, because we also have found in Suetonius and Appian that the duty of avenging Caesar was expanded to everyone, even though only the Senate made the vow.

The nature and the repercussions of the [Ed.: invented] vow, which is the subject of this discussion, is a unique case in Roman history, and it was due to this fact alone – its extraordinary conditions – that doubts were triggered about its authenticity. Consider the fact that the vow through which the Senate made itself protector and defender of Caesar was only valid for his lifetime and was binding only for the Senate, whereas the vow from the time of the expulsion of kingship was claimed to have been a vow that was binding on the entire populace for all of eternity!

Let me turn now to examine the validity of the *lex Valeria Publicolae*. Here, we need to keep in mind that it is a law that was applied in later Roman history several times, e.g., against extraordinary magistrates. I want to begin again with the accounts, first Livy:

> *Latae deinde leges ... ante amnes de provocatione adversus magistratur ad populum sacrandoque cum bonis capite eius qui regni occupandi consilia inisset gratae in vulgus leges fuere.*

> Laws were then proposed ... above all, the law about appealing from the magistrates to the people, and the one that pronounced a curse on the life and property of a man who should plot to make himself king, were welcome to the commons[51]

Next, Dionysius:

---

[51] Livy, *History of Rome*, 2.8.

ἕνα μὲν (νόμο ἔθετο) ἐν ᾧ διαρρήδην ἀπεῖπεν, ἄρχοντα μηδένα εἶναι Ῥωμαίων, ὃς ἂν μὴ παρὰ τοῦ δήμου λάβῃ τὴν ἀρχήν, θάνατον ἐπιθεὶς ζημίαν, ἐάν τις παρὰ ταῦτα ποιῇ καὶ τὸν ἀποκτείναντα τινὰ ποιῶν ἀθῷον.

He [Valerius] also introduced most beneficent laws ... by one of these he expressly forbade that anyone should be magistrate over the Romans who did not receive the office from the people; and he fixed as the death penalty for transgressing this law, and granted impunity to the one who should kill any such transgressor.[52]

Then follows the law about the right of appeal (*provocatio*); it contains the additional information that Valerius was given the nickname "*Publicola*" – the people's friend – because of these laws. Now, Plutarch:

δεύτερος ὁ τοὺς ἀρχὴν ἀναλαβόντας, ἣν ὁ δῆμος οὐκ ἔδωκεν, ἀποθνήσκειν κελεύων ...... - ἔγραψε γὰρ νόμον ἄνευ κρίσεως κτεῖναι διδόντα τὸν βουλόμενον τυραννεῖν, κτείναντα δὲ φόνου καθαρὸν ἐποίησεν, εἰ παράσχοιτο τοῦ ἀδικήματος τοὺς ἐλέγχους.

A second [law] made it a capital offense to assume a magistracy which the people had not bestowed ... For he enacted a law by which anyone who sought to make himself tyrant might be slain without trial and the slayer should be free from blood-guilt if he produced the proofs of the crime.[53]

Here, we see the same law from both Dionysius and Plutarch, only in different words. The Romans considered as kings or tyrants even those who occupied a special status in the state for a longer time. Compare with Cicero, *De Re Publica* 2.49:

nostri quidem omnes reges vocitaverunt qui soli in populos perpetuam potestatem haberent. itaque et Sp. Cassius et M. Manlius et Sp. Maelius regnum occupere voluisse dicti sunt.

... we Romans have always given the name of king to all who exercise for life sole authority over a nation. Thus, for example, it has been said that Spurius Cassius, Marcus Manlius, and Spurius Maelius attempted to win the kingship, and recently ... [Ed.: lines missing]

---

[52]Dionysius, *Roman Antiquities*, 5.19.
[53]Plutarch, *Life of Publicola*, 11.12.

The reports about this are even thinner than the reports about the vow. We can find other issues of the *lex Valeria Publicola* in abundance, but we only can find three indications of the law "*de sacrando ...*" Cicero naturally fails us here again, even more clearly than before. Similar to all the other sources he lists the aims of Publicola, records how he tries to evade the suspicion that he strives for the crown, and then continues:

> *idemque, in quo fuit publicola maxime, legem ad populum tulit eam, quae centruiatis comitiis prima lata est, ne quis magistratus civem Romanum adversus provocationem necaret neve verberaret.*

> It was the same man who, by an act whereby he shows himself in the highest sense "the people's friend" proposed to the citizens that first law passed by the centuriate assembly, which forbade any magistrate to execute or scourge a Roman citizen in the face of an appeal.[54]

After that follows the *lex Valeria Horatia*: "*ne quis magistratus sine provocatione crearetur*" [no magistrate not subject to appeal shall be elected], and then the other actions of the Publicola are listed, similar to the other authors.

Why does Cicero ignore a law that in his own eyes must have been more important than the right to appeal and all the others? Why is the law about the vow missing from *De Legibus* when it should have been the primary one because it was fundamental to the Republic?[55] Further, Livy, in addition, emphasizes clearly, "*ante omnes*" [above all], that both mentioned laws would have been suitable to lend popularity to Valerius's *Publicola* and that especially through the *lex sacrata* he could demolish the allegations – that he aspired to autocratic rule – in the best way. Again we can assume with certainty that Cicero didn't know about such a law at all, and that he couldn't have known it, because his sources and the tradition didn't know it either.

The law rules that anyone who undertakes an action that could bring the Republican constitution to a fall displeases the gods,[56] and that his belongings would be given to the temples. The perpetrator would then

---

[54] Cicero, *De Re Publica*, 2.53.
[55] cf. Cicero, *De Legibus*, 2.58; Cicero, *Academica*, 2.13; Cicero, *De Haruspicum Responso*, 16.
[56] Mommsen, *Römisches Staatsrecht*, p. 904, p. 900.

be declared an outlaw and anyone could kill him with impunity. That there would be no trial is not implied here even though the punishment has a religious character.[57] That is the wording of the law in Livy, and that in turn probably also was the wording in his own source. Dionysius and Plutarch have additions that cannot be found in Livy, which make the law appear even stranger. The Greek reports mingle things[58] that are strictly separated in Roman jurisprudence: "The lawfully regulated criminal trial against anyone who aspires to kingship and the sworn insurance to never again tolerate any king, with the consequences of being declared an outlaw."

Again we are dealing with a falsification that is motivated by the intention to give a juridical defense to the murder of Caesar in addition to the religious defense, and to protect the perpetrators from pursuit. Only this time, the falsifier has formulated it similar to the decrees about the abolition of the decemvirate and the rejection of the Sullan-Caesarian [Ed.: type of] dictatorship.[59][60] It was declared in those [Ed.: decrees] that everyone who introduced a magistrate who was above the law – i.e., also above the law of appeal (*provocatio*) – was unlawful. Livy himself calls this law – passed during the abolition of the decemvirate – a *lex nova*, so it seems he entirely forgot the "basic law of the Republic", as Mommsen

---

[57]Mommsen, *Römisches Strafrecht*, p. 553, note 1, p. 902.

[58]Mommsen, *Römisches Staatsrecht*, p. 14, note.

[59]In 452 BC the plebeians and patricians of Rome agreed to the appointment of a commission of ten men to write up a code of law defining the principles of Roman administration; during the *decemviri*'s term in office, all other magistracies would be suspended, and their decisions were not subject to appeal. They submitted to the *Comitia Centuriata* a code of laws in ten headings, which was passed. The success of the Decemvirate prompted the appointment of a second college of *decemviri* for 450 BC. This second set added two more headings to their predecessors' ten, completing the Law of the Twelve Tables (*Lex Duodecim Tabularum*), which formed the centerpiece of the Roman constitutions for the next several centuries. Nevertheless, this Decemvirate's rule became increasingly violent and tyrannical. When the Decemvirate's term of office expired, the *decemviri* refused to leave office or permit successors to take office. Appius Claudius is said to have made an unjust decision which would have forced a young woman named Verginia into prostitution or as Appius's personal slave, prompting her father to kill her, and this travesty caused an uprising against the Decemvirate; the *decemviri* resigned their offices in 449 BC, and the ordinary magistrates (*magistratus ordinarii*) were re-instituted. [Ed.]

[60]Mommsen, *Römisches Staatsrecht*, p. 662; Cicero, *De Re Publica*, 2 31 and 54; Livy, *History of Rome*, 3.55.5.

called it. This strengthens our suspicion even more that we are dealing with a later invention.

Now, Caesar already had been subject to the previously mentioned laws, but there must have been more to it, if, during the birth of the Republic, there was a new regulation that explicitly demanded the murder of a tyrant by good patriots.

If I really believe that I have identified the *lex Valeria Publicola* as an anti-Caesarian falsification, then, to avoid certain criticism, I must also introduce something into this discussion that usually is called the Conference of the Vow and the Law, by which I refer to the murder of Spurius Maelius by Servilius Ahala.[61] Mommsen has assembled the original story of this event from the later ingredients found in the version that was transmitted by Piso[62] and the annalists who followed him.

If the vow and the law were indeed a historical fact, then Ahala – who, according to the ancient report, murdered the tyrant Maelius – was a real patriot, because he **only obeyed a law** which could be considered to be the foundation of the Republic. Mommsen recognizes this and adds: "That the sacralization occurs through the act itself, and not through the words of a judge, corresponds to the [Ed.: later] common interpretation of this law." However, it appears that, in the sources mentioned, such a murder was still considered "politically and legally offensive", which could only be the case if the Romans didn't know of any vow or any sacralization-law. Otherwise, Servilius Ahala[63] would have been represented as

---

[61] Mommsen, *Römische Forschungen*, II, p. 205.

[62] Lucius Calpurnius Piso Frugi (sometimes Censorinus) was a Roman consul in 133 BC, and a historian. He was author of the Annales, seven books about history of Rome from its beginning to Piso's time. Livy considered him a less reliable source than Fabius Pictor, because Piso tended to moralize and idealize history. The early nineteenth-century historian, Barthold Georg Niebuhr, wrote that Piso was the first Roman historian to introduce systematic forgeries. [Ed.]

[63] Gaius Servilius Structus Ahala was a 5th-century BC politician of ancient Rome, considered by many later writers to have been a hero. His fame rested on the contention that he saved Rome from Spurius Maelius in 439 BC by killing him with a dagger concealed under an armpit. This may be less historical fact and more etiological myth, invented to explain the Servilian cognomen *Ahala/Axilla*, which means "armpit" and is probably of Etruscan origin. This is mentioned by several later writers as an example of ancient Roman heroism and is frequently referred to by Cicero in terms of the highest admiration; but was regarded as a case of murder at the time. Ahala was brought to trial and only escaped condemnation

innocent and unpunished and would have been lauded for his deed. Later he indeed was celebrated as a tyrant-murderer; and it is known from history that that his example was used later to bolster and encourage his descendant Brutus. It was the precedent of a tyrant-murder, and as such it has come across in Roman history, even though the report with all its details "is an invented falsification in an aristocratic sense".[64]

But in order to achieve that goal, to justify it, they – [Ed.: some falsifier of history] – had to give a different character to this issue. The deed of Servilius Ahala was altered to appear less like the deed of a single man by the expedient of involving the whole Senate in it. The story was changed so that the actions and deeds of Spurius Maelius[65] – indicating that he aspired to become a king – were reported to the Senate, which then rebuked the consuls because they ignored such doings. In their defense it was said that they didn't have the power to effectively change anything[66] since they were hindered by the law of appeal (*provocatio*), and thus "*opus esse non forti solum viro, sed etiam libero exsolutoque legum vinclis*"[67][68] After saying this, Lucius Quinctius Cincinnatus was appointed dictator and he then took Servilius as *magister equitum*. The latter attempted to bring Spurius Maelius before the court of the dictator, and because he refused, he was stabbed down by Ahala there and then.

> ... bespattered with his blood and guarded by a company of young nobles, [Ahala] returned to the dictator and reported that Maelius, having been summoned to appear before him, had repulsed the attendant and was rousing up the populace when he received the pun-

---

by going into voluntary exile. Livy passes over this, and only mentions that a bill was brought in three years afterwards, in 436 BC, by another Spurius Maelius, a tribune, for confiscating the property of Ahala, but that it failed. Sources: Cicero, *in Catilinam* 1, *Pro Milone* 3, *De Senectute* 16; Valerius Maximus, 5.3.2; Cicero, *De Re Publica* 1.3, *De Domo Sua* 32; Livy, *History of Rome* 4.21. [Ed.]

[64]Mommsen, *Römische Forschungen*, II, p. 199.
[65]Livy, *History of Rome*, 3.12.6; 13.8; 11.11.
[66]Ibid., 2.29.10.
[67]"but Quinctius said that the consuls were blamed unjustly, for, constrained by the laws of appeal, which had been enacted in order to break down power in their office as they had will to punish so heinous an offence in the way it deserved. There was need, he continued, of a man, and one who was not only brave, but free and unfettered by the laws."
[68]Livy, *History of Rome*, 4.13.11–12.

ishment he had deserved. Whereat the dictator exclaimed, "Well done, Gaius Servilius; you have delivered the commonwealth!"

Then, as the crowd was in a turmoil, not knowing what to think of the deed, he bade convoke them to an assembly. There he asserted that Maelius had been justly slain, even though he had been innocent of plotting to make himself king, since he had been cited before the dictator by the master of the horse and had not obeyed. ... planning violence to avoid undergoing trial, he had been repressed by violence.[69]

[Ed. inserted quotation]

This and similar versions dominate in our later texts, and also Cicero emphasizes that Spurius Maelius's killing had been ordered by the dictator.[70] In Livy's report we can see clearly that no law and no vow was brought forward to serve as a protection. Why did Quinctius Cincinnatus say: "*opus esse ... viro ... exsoluto vinclis legum*" ["there was need of a man unfettered by the laws"], when they could have used a much more powerful argument? Regarding this, Quinctius defended himself in a long monologue, but he only used arguments that had previously been used against the kingship, and never alludes at all to the *lex Valeria* or any [Ed.: Republic-founding] vow.

From all this we can see clearly that Servilius's fame rested merely on the fact that he had committed an "approved" murder – not more and not less – which could not be vindicated by any law, and where the only excuse was that he acted according to the example of the predecessors out of concern for freedom. That explains why the altered version has taken such a strong hold in the tradition, and why nobody has ever questioned the invention of the vow and even fewer have seen this process as a necessary consequence of these regulations.

Livy and Dionysius do not mention with a single word that they are convinced that the ancient vow would have justified this murder, and even though Mommsen says that this is evident, I cannot find any evidence of it. If the falsifier – the origin of the historical lies under discussion – was an annalist, then he only reproduced the story in a simple format, as it is written by Piso; because Dionysius talks about Piso "and the other annalists" (see above). If [Ed.: the falsifier] used his falsely introduced

---

[69] Livy, *History of Rome*, 4.14–15.
[70] Cicero, *De Senectute*, 16 (36).

regulations as a legal justification for the murder of Spurius Maelius, this cannot be easily decided on the basis of the currently available historical accounts. In any event, later historians have used this particular story because its ingredients were more interesting and more diversified and corresponded more closely with the common trend. So, this episode also argues for the point that the vow and the law are later inventions, unless, of course, a contradiction is found.

Now I would like to mention another falsification of a similar kind that was proven[71] by Otto Seeck. Consul Flaminius had made enemies with the Senate due to his former political behavior[72]; his plans had been thwarted several times by the Senate and because he feared that he would be locked into the city by invented auspices or other similar methods he left Rome as a civilian without the appropriate rituals to become consul. By lot he was assigned the army that was located at the Po. Via edict, he ordered the army to relocate to Ariminium at the 15th of March, where he intended to start his consulate. The Senate, upon learning of his plans, threatened

---

[71] Seeck, "Der Bericht des Livius über den Winter 218/17 v. Chr.", p. 116.

[72] Gaius Flaminius Nepos was a politician and consul of the Roman Republic in the 3rd century BC. He was the greatest popular leader to challenge the authority of the Senate before the Gracchi a century later. In the aftermath of the First Punic War, Flaminius, a *novus homo*, was the leader of a reform movement that sought to reorganize state land in Italy. As tribune of the plebs in 232 BC, he passed a plebiscite that divided the Ager Gallicus (the land south of Ariminum, which had been conquered from the Gauls decades before) and gave it to poor families whose farms had fallen into ruin during the war. The Senate was opposed to this and he did not consult them, contrary to the constitution and tradition. In 223 Flaminius was elected consul for the first time, and with Publius Furius Philus he forced the Gauls to submit to Rome, creating the province of Cisalpine Gaul. In 221 Flaminius was *magister equitum* to Marcus Minucius Rufus, then in 220 chosen as censor along with Lucius Aemilius Papus. During his term he arranged for the *Via Flaminia* to be built from Rome to Ariminum, established colonies at Cremona and Placentia, reorganized the Centuriate Assembly to give the poorer classes more voting power, and built the *Circus Flaminius* on the *Campus Martius*. In 218, while serving in the Senate, he was the only senator to support the *Lex Claudia*, which prohibited senators from participating in overseas trade. In 217, during the Second Punic War and the invasion of Italy by Hannibal, he was re-elected consul with Gnaeus Servilius Geminus, in what was considered a rebuke of the Senate's prosecution of the war. Flaminius raised four new legions and marched north to meet Hannibal, but was ambushed at Lake Trasimene. The army was destroyed and Flaminius was killed on 27 April 217 BC. [Ed.]

to recall him. They sent envoys who were supposed to bring him back but failed. Seeck has proven that this report from Livy cannot correspond to facts. To illuminate the tendency for this falsification, [Ed.: Seeck] refers to a similar episode in Caesar's life, who, aged 49, also left Rome as a civilian to start a consulate in Brundisium. Compare the details with the mentioned essay.

I doubt that these mentioned falsifications exhaust everything that can be found in Roman history that reflect anti-Caesarian tendencies [Ed.: propaganda]. When I reflect on the image of the last king of Rome, and when I see similarities to Caesar in it, then I am fully aware that I must not claim absolute belief in it. But in relation to all that has been previously mentioned, my perspective gains in likelihood, especially when we consider that the falsifier, who acted intentionally and was looking for contemporary parallels, must have focused on the last king from whom all hatred of the kingship originated. If he was able[73] to foist offensive acts of Scipio onto Caesar, then it must have been even easier for him to add negative aspects to a person who lived long before him, like Tarquinius, the Roman tyrant exemplar.

Even though Cicero mentions Tarquinius rather often, he actually reports fewer details about him than later historians, and he doesn't judge him harshly at all; and that is not likely due to any feeling of mercy; [Ed.: obviously, the Tarquinius Cicero knew was not the same Tarquinius that we know today thanks to later historians and falsifications, as is discussed here]. I want to add that it doesn't matter so much what actually Caesar did, but what accusations were made against him. The similarities are as follows:

1. Caesar surrounded himself with Spanish body guards, and that was only necessary to someone who claimed his position illegally.[74] About Tarqunius it is said:

   "*Conscius male quaerendi regni a se ipso adversus se exemplum capi posse, armatis corpus circumsaepsit*"

   Conscious that the precedent which he had set, of winning a throne by violence, might be used against himself, he surrounded himself with a guard.

---

[73] cf. Mommsen, *Römische Forschungen*.

[74] Appian, *Civil Wars*, 2.109; Suetonius, *Ceasar*, 86; Livy, *History of Rome*, 1.49.2.

2. Caesar so strikingly cared about the goodwill of the Transpadanians, who employed the Latin law, that allegations of selfish behavior were raised against him, because it was thought that he hoped that they would support him.[75] In Tarquinius it is the Latins that are backing him:

> *Latinorum sibi maxime gentem conciliabat, ut peregrinis quoque opibus tutior inter cives esset*[76]

> He made a special point of securing the Latin nation, that through his power and influence abroad he might be safer amongst his subjects at home.

He apparently did that repeatedly, but in the later parts of the story the only intention of Tarquinius was said to be to bring the Latins under the rule of Rome, and he did not hesitate to use force to achieve that. Contradicting himself, Livy later said:

> ... *necem machinatur, ut eundem terrorem, quo civium animos domi oppresserat, Latinis iniceret*

> ... in order that he might inspire the Latins with the same terror through which he had crushed the spirits of his subjects at home.

That is why the first motive must have been added later.

3. By decree of the Senate, Caesar obtained the power to decide about war and peace;[77] he used this power to represent the Senate and populace by his own person and issued decrees, to which he added names of senators:

> *omnia delata ad unum sunt, is utitur consilio ne suorum quidem, sed suo.*

> For authority of every kind has been committed to one man. He consults nobody but himself, not even his friends.[78]

---

[75]Dio, *Roman History*, 41.36.3; Suetonius, *Ceasar*, 8; Cicero, *Ad Atticum*, 7.7.6; 5.2; Cicero, *Ad Familiares*, 16.12.4; Caesar, *Civil War*, 3.87.4; cf. Schmidt, *Römisches Strafrecht*, p. 5.
[76]Livy, *History of Rome*, 1.49.8; 50; 51.1.
[77]Drumann, *Geschichte Roms*, p. 524; Dionysius, *Roman Antiquities*, 42.20.1.
[78]Cicero, *Ad Familiares*, 9.15.4; 4.9.2.

Tarquinius is accused of the same arbitrariness:

> ... *traditum a prioribus morem, de ombibus senatum consulendi solvit*

> For this king was the first to break with the custom handed down ... of consulting the Senate on all occasions, and governed the nation without other advice than that of his own household.

and

> *ut qui neque populi iussu neque auctoribus patribus regnaret* and ... *bellum, pacem, foedera, societates per se ipse, cum quibus voluit, iniussu populi ac senatus fecit, diremitqe.*[79]

> War, peace, treaties, and alliances were entered upon or broken off by the monarch himself, with whatever states he wished, and without the decree of people or Senate.

Here, the kingship seems to be limited, which, from a historic perspective, is not believable.[80] The accusations cannot hit Tarquinius. We may want to pay attention to the expressions "*populi iussu*" [by order or consent of the people] and "*iniussu populi ac senatus*" [by vote of the people or Senate], whereas surely only "*auctoritas*" [authority] can be applied to Tarquinius.

4. Caesar created a similar offense with his arbitrariness regarding the judiciary. Compare with Tarqunius:

> ... *cognitiones capitalium rerum sine consiliis per se solus exercebat.*

> To inspire terror ... he adopted the practice of trying capital causes by himself, without advisers ...[81]

This reproach is pointless since the king "sat in court for all private and criminal matters of law and absolutely ruled over life and death."[82]

---

[79]Livy, *History of Rome*, 1.497; Dionysius, *Roman Antiquities*, 4.41.
[80]cf. Mommsen, *Römische Geschichte*, I, p. 245; Schwegler, *Römische Geschichte*, I, p. 662.
[81]Livy, *History of Rome*, 1.49; Dionysius, *Roman Antiquities*, 4.41; Mommsen, *Römische Geschichte*, III, p. 494.
[82]Mommsen, *Römische Geschichte*, I, p. 62, p. 248; Mommsen, *Römisches Staatsrecht*, II, p. 12; Livy, *History of Rome*, 1.26.5.

5. Caesar made many enemies because he selected only a few men to be close advisors, and because, somewhat abruptly, he installed a secret advisory council, bypassing the administration as elected by the public.[83] Tarquinius also mentions: "*domesticis consiliis rem publicam administrabat*" [governed the nation without other advice than that of his own household.]. An attempt to find examples and evidence for these bad habits of Tarquinius naturally will be in vain.

It is clear that, apart from these listed "signs of the tyrant", common and typical tyrannical traits are absent in Tarquinius; the specific offenses to the Roman Republican spirit seem to be later ingredients. The assumption is obvious that – because Caesar threatened the Republican freedom – the kingship had to be described as more hateful than it actually had been, and this was done by exaggerating the terrors of the last regal period. One only has to think about the dark perspective that Cicero gives:

> *cadem video, ... regnum non modo Romano homini sed ne Persae cuiquam tolerabile.*

> For I foresee a massacre if he wins and an onslaught on private property and return of exiles and cancellation of debts and elevation of rapscallions to office and despotism worse than any Persian, let alone Roman, could endure.[84]

Cicero's whole essay is permeated by those pessimistic viewpoints. It didn't become that bad, but every Republican hated Caesar's aspiration towards autocratic rule. What could have been a better method to fight against him, than to establish similar intentions and similar bad habits for Tarquinius! Cicero never gave a detailed description of Tarquinius, as the later historians did, quite the opposite: he judged him in a very favorable manner.[85][86] Those **detailed characteristics** were created after Cicero,

---

[83] Tacitus, *Annals*, 12.60; Suetonius, *Ceasar*, 76; cf. Schmidt, *Römisches Strafrecht*; Livy, *History of Rome*, 1.49; Dionysius, *Roman Antiquities*, 4.41.
[84] Cicero, *Ad Atticum*, 7.8.
[85] "... we from the time when the kings were driven out have forgotten how to be slaves. And that Tarquinius, whom our ancestors expelled, was not either considered or called cruel or impious, but only The Proud. That vice which we have often borne in private individuals, our ancestors could not endure even in a king." [Ed.]
[86] Cicero, *Philippica*, 3.8 and 9; Cicero, *Pro C. Rabirio perduellionis reo*.

and the originator likely is the same person who carries the responsibility for the other falsifications. It seems that a way had been found to fight against the usurper, who seemed to create similar circumstances to those which caused the fall of the kingship.

Again we are confronted with the question, who created those falsifications? They must have been created after 44, and, as mentioned earlier, later historians must have drawn from one, single source. What is the pool for our selection? Who wrote a historical essay between 44 and 30?

Firstly, we have Q. Aelius Tubero to consider. About his life and his literary work we know[87] the following: In the civil wars he fought with Pompeius against Caesar, who afterwards reprieved him, after which he seemed to be on good terms with Caesar. He dedicated an essay to the Caesarian Oppius.[88] We do not know if he dedicated himself again to the Republican Party after Caesar was murdered.[89] In the 30s he published an annal, consisting of 14 books which covered the time period from the beginning of Rome until perhaps his own time; I say "perhaps" because, according to Klebs, it is not entirely unlikely that the statements of the Fragments that relate to Caesar do not stem from the historical writing, but from a single writing about Caesar called *Liber ad C. Oppium*, which I already mentioned.[90]

Oppius also wrote a book about Caesar; and Suetonius, who especially liked to quote from obscure writings, probably had access to work from Tubero. It is uncertain if Tubero[91] copied in full the historical writing of his father; but the mentioned falsifications could not have been part of the father's writings, because, according to Cicero, *ad Quintum Fratrem* 1.1.10, he already had worked on the history in 60 BC[92] and the lies were

---

[87] Smith, *Dictionary of Greek and Roman Biography and Mythology*; Klebs in Pauly and Wissowa, *Realencyclopädie der Classischen Altertumswissenschaft*, p. 534.

[88] Gellius, *Attic Nights*, 6.9 and 11; Peter, *Historicorum Romanorum*, I, pp. CC-CLXI/313, Fragments 6–7.

[89] cf. Klebs in Pauly and Wissowa, *Realencyclopädie der Classischen Altertumswissenschaft*, I, p. 537.

[90] mentioned by Gellius, *Attic Nights*, 7.19.

[91] Pauly and Wissowa, *Realencyclopädie der Classischen Altertumswissenschaft*, I, p. 694; Dionysius, *Roman Antiquities*, 1.80; Cicero, *Ad Quintum Fratrem*, 1.1.3 (10).

[92] "... you have in the persons of your *legati* men likely to have a regard for their own reputation. Of these in rank, position, and age Tubero is first; who, I think, particularly as he is a writer of history, could select from his own Annals many

created much later. Can we then assume that Q. Aelius Tubero has added the lies [Ed.: in question] to history? The only reason we might consider him is the period in which he lived. But there are more reasons that speak against him being the author of the falsification. First of all, we don't have any judgment from later writers that would enable us to assume that. The only [Ed.: judgment] we know of comes from Dionysius,[93] and according to it, he was a ... «δεινὸς ἀνὴρ καὶ περὶ τὴν συναγωγὴν τῆς ἱστορίας ἐπιμελής.» [shrewd man and careful in collecting his historical facts].

From his fragments we can conclude only very little about the historical accuracy of his work. For us, it is crucial only that he seems to have been quoted so little.

Livy, Dionysius, Plutarch, and Appian all contain the falsifications.[94] Livy mentions him thrice, and it seems that he mentions him often in context with Licinius Macer.[95][96] Dionysius quoted him only once. Plutarch and Appian not at all. So we cannot talk here about any extensive usage.

The other bits are so scarce (13 fragments in Peter)[97] that we can say with certainty that he didn't have a lot of influence on the historical

---

whom he would like and would be able to imitate." [Ed.]

[93] Dionysius, *Roman Antiquities*, 1.80.

[94] cf. Peter, *Historicorum Romanorum*, Fr.

[95] Macer wrote a history of Rome in 16 books. The work is now lost, but from Livy and Dionysius, who both used it, we know that it began with the founding of the city, and that Pyrrhus appeared in book 2. Livy casts doubt on Macer's reliability, suggesting that he misrepresented events in order to glorify the Licinii, but notes that he quotes original sources, such as the Linen Rolls. Livy, *History of Rome*, 7.9.5. [Ed.]

[96] "I find in Macer Licinius that the same consuls were re-elected for the following year – Julius for the third time and Verginius for the second. Valerius Antias and Q. Tubero give M. Manlius and Q. Sulpicius as the consuls for that year. In spite of this discrepancy Tubero and Macer both claim the authority of the "Linen Rolls"; both admit that in the ancient historians it was asserted that there were military tribunes that year. Licinius considers that we ought unhesitatingly to follow the "Linen Rolls"; Tubero has not made up his mind. But amongst the many points obscure through lapse of time, this also is left unsettled." Livy, *History of Rome*, 4.23.

[97] Hermann Peter, *Historicorum Romanorum Reliquiae*: two-volume collection of scholarly editions of fragmentary Roman historical texts edited by Hermann Peter and published between 1870 and 1914. Peter published the Latin editions of these texts, without translation and with introductions in Latin; for the greatest part of the twentieth century, this was the standard edition of such texts. [Ed.]

record. However, if we look at the meaning of the falsifications [Ed.: taken together with the time of writing that we can infer from the meaning], then we are forced to decide that he must be the author. Who else could it have been?

Nobody other than Valerius Antias.[98] But in order to regard him as the source of the falsifications, we have to get rid of an obstacle in our way, and that is the common agreement about the dating of his life. Here I want to adhere very closely to the transmitted fragments in order to show that his work could not have been written in the time of Sulla [Ed.: as is generally assumed], but between 40 and 30 BC.

> *Ventustior Sisenna fuit Caelius, aequalis Sisennae Rutilius Claudiusque Quadrigarius et Valerius Antias.*
>
> Sisenna, the author of the *Histories*, was still a young man. His works on the Civil Wars and the Wars of Sulla were published several years later. Caelius was earlier than Sisenna, while Rutilius, Claudius Quadrigarius and Valerius Antias were his contemporaries.[99]

With these words, Velleius Paterculus[100] gives us the relative times of the three historians in question. The mentioned Rutilius was praetor in

---

[98] Valerius Antias (1st century BC) was an ancient Roman annalist whom Livy mentions as a source. No complete works of his survive but from the 65 fragments said to be his in the works of other authors it has been deduced that he wrote a chronicle of ancient Rome in at least 75 books. Livy criticizes his exaggerated numbers of killed and captured enemies in the Roman wars. Sometimes he seems to have invented even battles. Antias related his stories very long-winded and filled with sensationalism to entertain his readers. He embroidered the mostly short accounts of older historians with dramatic details and also recounted legends and miracles. He falsified the report about the trials of the Scipio brothers (compare Livy, *History of Rome*, 38.50–60) and seems to have invented high offices and deeds of members of his house, the *gens* Valeria, who lived in the early Roman Republic because there were no reliable sources about these early times, which could have disproved his assertions. Antias gave a rationalistic account about the discovery of the coffins with the books of King Numa, because he had the coffins uncovered by rain and not by excavation like in the older tradition. Howard, Albert A. (1906). "Valerius Antias and Livy". *Harvard studies in classical philology* (Cambridge: Harvard University) 18: 161–182. [Ed.]

[99] Peter, *Historicorum Romanorum*, I, p. 287; Velleius Paterculus, *Roman History*, 2.9.

[100] Velleius Paterculus, c. 19 BC–c. AD 31 – a Roman historian, also known simply as Velleius. He served for eight years (from AD 4) in Germany and Pannonia under

the year 111, and allegedly was a contemporary of Sisenna, who took the praetorship in 78,[101] i.e., despite the 30 years in between. This fact ought to immediately make us suspicious regarding the claim. If Peter had inspected the quoted sentences from Velleius a bit more closely, he would have become even more suspicious. Because there we can also read:

> *celebre et Lucilii nomen fuit, qui sub P. Africano Numantino nello eques militaverat. Quo quidem tempore iuvenes adhuc Jugurtha ac Marius sub eodem Africano militantes in iisdem costris didicere, quae pastea in contrariis facerent. historiarum auctor iam tum Sisenna erat iuvenis, sed opus belli civilis Sullanique post aliquot annos ab eo seniore editum est.*

The famous knight, Lucilius, served under Scipio Africanus[102] at the siege of Numantia (in 134 BC) along with the young Jugurtha[103] who was serving under Marius [one of Africanus's generals]. Sisenna, the historian, was a young man even then and published his work on the Sullan Civil War some years later.

If we allow that Sisenna was age 20 – three years after the end of the Numantine War (130), then he would have – *post aliquot annos* – published the writings about the civil war and Sulla at least 50 years later [Ed.: since it did not begin until the year 83 BC] and would – no doubt – have happily become praetor at age 72! With such a chronology, it is not hard to imagine what the situation must be regarding the contemporaneity of Claudius Quadrigarius[104] and Valerius Antias. Even though Peter partly recognizes the general unreliability of the chronology of Velleius

---

Tiberius. For his services he was rewarded with the quaestorship in AD 8, and, together with his brother, with the praetorship in AD 15. He was still alive in AD 30, for his history contains many references to the consulship of M. Vinicius in that year. It has been conjectured that he was put to death in AD 31 as a friend of Sejanus. [Ed.]

[101] Mommsen, *Corpus Inscriptionum Latinarum*, I, p. 111; Peter, *Historicorum Romanorum*, I, p. CCCXXIII.

[102] Publius Cornelius Scipio Aemilianus Africanus Numantinus (185–129 BC). [Ed.]

[103] Jugurthen (c. 160–104 BC) was a King of Numidia, born in Cirta (modern-day Constantine). [Ed.]

[104] Quintus Claudius Quadrigarius, Roman annalist, wrote a history, in at least 23 books, which began with the conquest of Rome by the Gauls (c. 390 BC) and continued to the time of Sulla (Fragment 84; 82 BC). Along with annalist Valerius Antias, Livy freely used Quadrigarius as a major source in part of his work (from the sixth book

Paterculus, he nevertheless thinks that the lifetimes of Quadrigarius and Antias are correct, only because it is referenced elsewhere. He refers to Gellius 15.1.5 and 10.1.3. But from these sources we only conclude that Quadrigarius did not die **before** the events that are chronicled there.[105]

Because we are missing the evidence about how far his story reaches, this hint doesn't help us.

Next, Peter refers to the chronology given by Fronto[106] and cites:

historiam quoque scripsere – Pictor incondite, Claudius lipide,

---

onwards). A substantial fragment is preserved in Aulus Gellius, *Attic Nights*, 9.13. The fragments of his work are collected in H. Peter, *Historicorum Romanorum* (I, pp. 205–237). [Ed.]

[105] In Peter. Quadrigarius Fragment 81: "*In eo libro scriptum inveni cum oppugnaret L. Sulla in terra Attica Piraeum et contra Archelaus regis Mithridati praefectus ex eo oppido propugnaret, turrim ligneam ...*" [In this book, I have found L. Sylla in Attica and Piraeus besieging King Mithridates officer, Archelaus, with a wooden tower ...] Fragment 82: "*O. Claudium in libro undecimo C. Marium cretum 'septimo' consulem disisse*" [In the 11th book of O. Claudium, Marius is consul for the 7th time ...].

[106] Marcus Cornelius Fronto (c. 100–170), Roman grammarian, rhetorician and advocate, was born in the Berber city Cirta in Numidia. Educated at Rome, he soon gained such renown as an advocate and orator as to be reckoned inferior only to Cicero. He amassed a large fortune, erected magnificent buildings and purchased the famous gardens of Maecenas. Antoninus Pius, hearing of his fame, appointed him tutor to his adopted sons Marcus Aurelius and Lucius Verus. Until 1815, the only extant works ascribed (erroneously) to Fronto were two grammatical treatises, De nominum verborumque differentiis and Exempla elocutionum (the latter being really by Arusianus Messius). In that year, Angelo Mai discovered in the Ambrosian library at Milan a palimpsest manuscript, on which had been originally written some of Fronto's letters to his imperial pupils and their replies; four years later Mai found several more sheets from this manuscript in the Vatican. These palimpsests had originally belonged to the famous convent of St Columbanus at Bobbio, and had been written over by the monks with the acts of the First Council of Chalcedon. The collection also contains treatises on eloquence, some historical fragments, and literary trifles on such subjects as the praise of smoke and dust, of negligence, and a dissertation on Arion. In addition, a fragment of a speech is preserved by Minucius Felix (*Octavius* 9.6–7) in which Fronto accuses the Christians of incestuous orgies. Marcus Aurelius credits Fronto with teaching him about the vices of tyranny and the lack of affection in the Roman upper class (1.11); since the former were commonplaces, there may be a concealed reference to life under Hadrian, whom Fronto retrospectively claims to have feared rather than loved, but the latter is borne out by the master's remark that there is no Latin equivalent for the Greek *philóstorgos*, meaning "affectionate". [Ed.]

Antias invenuste, Sisenna longinque[107]
  wrote a history – incoherent Pictor, fat Claudius, ugly Antias, distant Sisenna

Here however we have the same chronology as in Velleius; but how little binding that is for us we can see when Fronto writes: "Sallustius structe"[108] (where Peter sets the dash), i.e., where he mentions the most recently living historian. This correction alone not only is enough to make Peter's argumentation illusory at this point, but in addition I want to emphasize Fronto's just mentioned sentence where he lists the writers in the following order: "Lucilius,[109] Albucius,[110] Lucretinus,[111] Pacuvius,[112] Ac-

---

[107] Peter, *Historicorum Romanorum reliquiae*, p. CCLXXXVII.
[108] Fronto, *Epistula ad Verum*, 1.1, p. 14.
[109] The earliest Roman satirist, of whose writings only fragments remain. The dates assigned by Jerome for his birth and death are 148 BC and 103 BC or 102 BC. But it is impossible to reconcile the first of these dates with other facts recorded of him, and the date given by Jerome must be due to an error, the true date being about 180 BC. His sister was Lucilia, being the mother of Roman Politician Sextus Pompeius and the paternal grandmother of Roman Triumvir Pompey. It is in the highest degree improbable that Lucilius served in the army at the age of fourteen; it is still more unlikely that he could have been admitted into the familiar intimacy of Scipio and Laelius at that age. It also seems an impossibility that between the ages of fifteen and nineteen – i.e., between 133 BC and 129 BC, the year of Scipio's death – he could have come before the world as the author of an entirely new kind of composition which demands maturity of judgment and experience. The true date of his birth must be around 180 BC. [Ed.]
[110] Titus Albucius (praetor c. 105 BC) was satirized by Lucilius, whose lines upon him are preserved by Cicero who thought he was shallow. He unsuccessfully accused Mucius Scaevola, the augur, of maladministration (*repetundae*) in his province. He was accused in 103 BC of *repetundae* by Gaius Julius Caesar (the elder), and condemned. [Ed.]
[111] Titus Lucretius Carus (c. 99–c. 55 BC) was a Roman poet and philosopher. His only known work is the epic philosophical poem *De Rerum Natura* about the beliefs of Epicureanism, and which is translated into English as *On the Nature of Things* or "On the Nature of the Universe". In a letter by Cicero to his brother Quintus in February 54 BC, Cicero said that: "The poems of Lucretius are as you write: they exhibit many flashes of genius, and yet show great mastership." By this time, both Cicero and his brother had read *De Rerum Natura*, and so might have many other Romans. There is a sudden end to Book 6 during a description of the plague at Athens. The poem appears to have been published without a final revision, possibly due to its author's death. If this is true, Lucretius must have been dead by 54 BC. [Ed.]
[112] Marcus Pacuvius (c. 29 April 220–7 February 130 BC) was the greatest of the tragic

cius,[113] Ennius."[114] Obviously, listing the names chronologically was not important for him and he only lists them in an arbitrary way – whoever came first into his mind. In addition, he was separated from the annals in question by 150 to 200 years. The assumption that Quadrigarius is supposed[115] to have written before Sisenna, who died in 67 – at the approximate age of 80 – is completely unreliable. And in the same way we cannot maintain that Valerius Antias lived during the same period and thus could be called a contemporary of Sisenna just because his name is sorted later.

If we look for other evidence and ask who mentioned Antias first and quoted from him first, then we see that Peter believes that he can deduce from Fragments 10, 18, and 17 that Varro cited him first; the reason being that the name "Antias" appears in such a close connection with the name "Varro" that his name and his citations seem to be copied from comparative writings of Varro. The fragments in question are:

- Fragment 10:

    Ancum praenomen Varro e Sabinis translatum putat, Val. Antias scribit, quod cubitum vitiosum habuerit, qui Graece vocatur

---

poets of ancient Rome prior to Lucius Accius. He was the nephew and pupil of Ennius. Cicero, who frequently quotes from him with great admiration, appears (*De Optimo Genere Oratorum* 1) to rank him first among the Roman tragic poets, as Ennius among the epic, and Caecilius among the comic poets. [Ed.]

[113]Lucius Accius (170–c. 86 BC), or Lucius Attius, a Roman tragic poet and literary scholar. The son of a freedman, Accius was born at Pisaurum in Umbria, in 170 BC. The year of his death is unknown, but he must have lived to a great age, since Cicero (born 106 BC, hence 64 years younger) speaks of having conversed with him on literary matters. [Ed.]

[114]Quintus Ennius (c. 239–c. 169 BC) was a writer during the period of the Roman Republic, and is often considered the father of Roman poetry. The Epicharmus presented an account of the gods and the physical operations of the universe. In it, the poet dreamed he had been transported after death to some place of heavenly enlightenment. The Euhemerus presented a theological doctrine of a vastly different type in a mock-simple prose style modelled on the Greek of Euhemerus of Messene and several other theological writers. According to this doctrine, the gods of Olympus were not supernatural powers still actively intervening in the affairs of men, but great generals, statesmen and inventors of olden times commemorated after death in extraordinary ways. Ennius was said to have considered himself a reincarnation of Homer. [Ed.]

[115]Peter, *Historicorum Romanorum reliquiae*, CCCLXXXVI and CDV.

ἀγκών .

Ancus, the praenomen that Varro thinks was Sabine, Valerius Antias writes that the Greeks had a similar word which meant "crooked elbow ..."

- Fragment 18:

    nam ita institutm esse, ut centesimo quoque anno fierent (ludi saeculares). Id cum Antias aliique historici auctores scribunt, tum Varro.

    For that to be so, that might be one hundred years (Secular games). That historians and others with Antias write, then Varro ...

- Fragment 17:

    Valerio Maximo, ut Antias tradidit, inter alios honores domus quoque publice aedificata est in Palatio, cuius exitus, quo magis insignis esset, in publicum versus declinaretur, hoc est extra privatum aperiretur.

    Antias tells us that a house was built in the Palatium at public expense, among other honours, for M. Valerius Maximus; and the doors were made to swing outwards into the street, an extra touch of magnificence.

That is what Peter quotes as his evidence;[116] the addition is:

Varronem autem tradere, M. Valerio ... aedes in Palatio tributas, Junius Hyginus scripsit.

Junius Hyginus says that ... Varro passed to M. Valerius a house in the Palatium.

I had to quote the fragments to show how contrived the conclusion is that Varro has used Antias in them. Fragment 18 does not prove anything at all. Fragment 17 could be enough reason to assume that Varro has given his viewpoint as an addition to the one of Antias; but then, Valerius Maximus is expressing himself in a weird way when he says: "Varro

---

[116]Schwegler, *Römische Geschichte*, II, p. 89.

believes" ... and further: "Antias writes". It seems much more likely that the reader had two writings in front of him. Fragment 17 shows clearly that not much about this issue could have been found in Varro from Antias, because Asconius mentions both of them separately, which would have been useless if both viewpoints could have been found together in Varro. Thus, the assumption that Varro first used Antias is an uncertain hypothesis, and if someone absolutely wants to bring both into a mutual context, then we can argue by the same token that, conversely, Antias used Varro.

That is the reason why only Dionysius and Livy remain as those who mentioned Antias first. Out of those two, Livy believes him to be so important and so influential that he mentions him most and probably uses him most,[117] even though he sometimes feels himself obligated to point out his mendacity. He does not speak often about the mendacity of the other sources. He does this because of the reasons argued by Krause, p. 269–270, Liebaldt, p. 19, and also to cause harm to his literary rival and to bring his work into discredit. Therefore, he must have been highly acclaimed in this time, and perhaps must have lived before Livy, so that such a harsh invective was needed to break his image.

For the older times he certainly was used a lot; because, according to Dionysius 1.6.5–1.7, the earlier annals dealt with the old history of Rome only rather summarily. This allegation could not hit Antias because he started elaborating only in the second book. How much Dionysius valued him can be seen in 1.7.5, and he took for granted as true many of his lies; because many of those [Ed.: lies] we never will be able to ascribe to him, and we can believe him when he protests against the suspicion that there are falsifications present.[118]

> I begin my history, then, with the most ancient legends, which the historians before me have omitted as a subject difficult to be cleared up without diligent study ... it is a combination of every kind, forensic, speculative and narrative, to the intent that it may afford satisfaction both to those who occupy themselves with political debates and to those who are devoted to philosophical speculations, as well

---

[117]Livy, *History of Rome*, 26.49; 33.10; 36.19; 38.23; 39.41; 44.13; cf. Krause, *Vitae Et Fragmenta Veterum Historicorum Romanorum*, p. 268; Liebaldt, *De Valerio Antiate, annalium scriptore*, p. 10.

[118]Dionysius, *Roman Antiquities*, 1.7.

as to any who may desire mere undisturbed entertainment in their reading of history. Such things, therefore, will be the subjects of my history and such will be its form.[119] [Ed.]

Also, Pliny would not have mentioned him so often if he hadn't held him in such a high regard. Under these circumstances, shouldn't we be astonished that Cicero never mentioned his name and his value? Certainly he did not know him and he could not have known him because his writings were published only after Cicero's death. In *De Legibus* 1.2.3–7, Cicero enumerates the names of the Roman historians without mentioning him. There we can find: "Fabius,[120] Cato,[121] Piso, Ennius, Vennonius,[122]

---

[119] Ibid., 1.8.

[120] Quintus Fabius Pictor (flourished c. 200 BC, some sources give his birth as possibly in 254 BC) was one of the earliest Roman historians and considered the first of the annalists. He was a senator who fought against the Gauls in 225 BC, and against Carthage in the Second Punic War. He was appointed to travel to the oracle at Delphi in 216 BC, for advice after the Roman defeat at the Battle of Cannae. [Ed.]

[121] Marcus Porcius Cato (234 BC, Tusculum–149 BC) was a Roman statesman, commonly referred to as Censorius (the Censor), Sapiens (the Wise), Priscus (the Ancient), or Major, Cato the Elder, or Cato the Censor (to distinguish him from his great-grandson, Cato the Younger). From the date of his Censorship (184 BC) to his death in 149 BC, Cato held no public office, but continued to distinguish himself in the Senate as the persistent opponent of the new ideas. He was struck with horror, along with many other Romans of the graver stamp, at the licence of the Bacchanalian mysteries, which he attributed to the influence of Greek manners; and he vehemently urged the dismissal of the philosophers (Carneades, Diogenes, and Critolaus), who came as ambassadors from Athens, on account of the dangerous nature of the views expressed by them. Cato is famous not only as statesman or soldier, but also as author. He was a historian, the first Latin prose writer of any importance, and the first author of a history of Italy in Latin. Some have argued that if it were not for the impact of Cato's writing, Latin might have been supplanted by Greek as the literary language of Rome. [Ed.]

[122] Roman historian of the late 2nd century BC (in Cicero, *De Legibus* 1.6); nothing is known of him as a person. His presumably annalistic work (*Annalists*) began with stories of the founding of Rome and the period of the kings (*Origo Gentis Romanae* 20.1; Dionysius, *Roman Antiquities* 4.15.1), but its scope and end point are unknown. Cicero felt the need of it in 46 BC in his literary work in Tusculum (Cicero, *Ad Atticus* 12.3.1). Fragments in Peter, *Historicorum Romanorum* I, pp. CCIX/142. [Ed.]

Antipater,[123] Clodius,[124] Asellio,[125] Macer,[126] Sisenna."[127] From this follows that he ignores the memoire-writers and also the historians writing in Greek, which explains the absence of Cn. Aufidius, C. Acilius, and U. Postumius. Fabius Pictor is mentioned because there existed a Latin translation of his work. This means that only Cassius Hemina, Tuditanus and Antias remain missing. It is also striking that Sempronius Asellio is amongst them, because he wrote about his own experiences.[128] But Cicero does not count him as a historical writer, and he does not deserve that because he had a special status amongst them; he did not so much intend to report only his experiences, but aspired to pragmatism under the influence of Polybius. He asks in Gellius:

> *nobis non modo satis esse video, quid factum esset, sed etiam quo consilio quaque ratione gesta essent demonstrare*

> For my part, I realize that it is not enough to make known what has been done, but that one should also show with what purpose and

---

[123] Lucius Coelius Antipater was a Roman jurist and historian. He is not to be confused with Coelius Sabinus, the Coelius of the Digest. He was a contemporary of C. Gracchus (b. c. 123); L. Crassus, the orator, was his pupil. He wrote a history of the Second Punic War, and composed Annales, which were epitomized by Brutus. He is occasionally quoted by Livy, who sometimes, with respectful consideration, dissents from his authority. It is manifest, however, from Cicero and Valerius Maximus that he was fond of relating dreams and portents. [Ed.]

[124] Quintus Claudius Quadrigarius. [Ed.]

[125] Publius Sempronius Asellio (c. 158–after 91 BC) was an early Roman historian and one of the first writers of historiographic work in Latin. He was a military tribune of P. Scipio Aemilianus Africanus at the siege of Numantia in Hispania in 134 BC. [Ed.]

[126] Gaius Licinius Macer (d. 66 BC) was an official and annalist of ancient Rome. A member of the ancient plebeian gens Licinia, he was tribune in 73 BC; Sallust mentions him agitating for the people's rights. He became praetor in 68, but in 66 Cicero succeeded in convicting him of bribery and extortion, upon which Macer committed suicide. [Ed.]

[127] Lucius Cornelius Sisenna (c. 120–67 BC) was a Roman soldier, historian, and annalist. He was killed in action during Pompey's campaign against pirates after the Third Mithridatic War. Sisenna had been commander of the forces on the coast of Greece. He was the author of a history in 23 books, all of which have been lost, save a few fragments. Sallust is said to have begun historical work as a continuation of Sisenna's. [Ed.]

[128] Nipperdey, "Zur Geschichte der röm. Historiographie"; Stelkens, "Der Römische Geschichtsschreiber Sempronius Asellio".

for what reason things were done.[129]

It is obvious why Cicero could not ignore him easily. But why then has he not mentioned the other three historians?

About Cassius Hemina[130] we can note the following: Cicero doesn't know him even in other places, and we cannot reproach him for this, since this annalist wasn't mentioned by Livy or Dionysius no other historians who wrote about this time, despite the fact no other writer dealt with the time period up to the Third Punic War.[131] His work was small and only consisted of five books. Pliny was the first to quote him.[132] Before Pliny, Varro may have used him also, to whom Macrobius, Solin, Censorinus, and Minucius Felix owe their citations directly or indirectly. Not a single historian of antiquity knew him or used him. When his name appears in Appian, then the word Κάσσιος [Cassius] is based on a conjecture. He is missing in Dionysius 1.11, as in Cicero, almost as the only missing one in the long assortment of historians. So it is easy to forgive Cicero for not knowing him and not mentioning him, because even the other historians do not notice him.

But what about Tuditanus[133]? It is questionable if he even wrote an

---

[129] Gellius, *Attic Nights*, 5.18.

[130] Lucius Cassius Hemina, Roman annalist, composed his annals in the period between the death of Terence and the revolution of the Gracchi. He wrote in Latin around 146 BC, including the earliest chronicle concerning the career of Mucius Scaevola. The fragments of his works have been edited by Peter in *Historicorum Romanorum Reliquiae*. [Ed.]

[131] Peter, *Historicorum Romanorum*, I, p. 108, Fragment 39.

[132] Pliny, *Natural History*, 32.20; 13.85. Münzer, *Beiträge zur Quellenkritik der Naturgeschichte des Plinius*, pp. 183, 189; Pauly and Wissowa, *Realencyclopädie der Classischen Altertumswissenschaft*, III^2, p. 1723.

[133] Gaius Sempronius Tuditanus was a politician and historian of the Roman Republic. He was consul in 129 BC. Cicero confused several times the younger Tuditanus with his father and was informed of his mistake by his friend Titus Pomponius Atticus in May 45 BC. Only a few fragments of his works have been preserved. Cicero emphasized his elegant style. In the internal Roman power struggles Tuditanus belonged to the Optimates and wrote a tendentious treatise on Roman constitutional law (*libri magistratuum*) in at least 13 books for the political support of his party. The *libri magistratuum* dealt with the intercalation, the appointment of the Plebeian Tribunes, the *nundinae* (market and feast days of the old Roman calendar), etc. [Ed.]

'annal' work. We only know that he wrote the title *libri magistratuum*,[134] because only this is mentioned. Next to it a purely historical work has been assumed because the contents of the existing fragments could not be well reconciled with the mentioned title. Conrad Cichorius has forcefully argued against these considerations.[135] The fragment which most clearly contains annalistic characteristics[136] was identified by him to not have come from Tuditanus. The three remaining fragments can rightfully be assumed to be part of the libri magistratuum, rather than assume a never-mentioned annalistic work. Now, Cichorius has proven with high likelihood that Tuditanus gave his work an antiquarian character, and in such a work the three fragments fit. Hence, Cicero could not have known them.

Now, how does it come that Cicero mentions his contemporary fellows Licinius Macer and Cornelius Sisenna, but not Antias? Both of them died in the year 67, the former one convicted[137] as a praetor by Cicero himself and driven to suicide. He certainly would know them well. But still, next to these persons he should not have missed a man of the importance of Valerius Antias, who must have had a large circle of readers in Rome. And even if he didn't mention him in his *De Legibus*, then at least there must have been a trace of him in his other writings. That the reputation of Valerius Antias was not minor can be seen in Dionysius 1.7.5, where he is put on the same level as men like Cato, Fabius Maximus, Licinius Macer, Calpurnius Piso, as one of the ἐπαινούμενοι ['approved' authors], as the οὐκ ἀφανεῖς ['not unseen']. Nevertheless there is no trace of it in Cicero, who certainly could not have left out a literary phenomenon of such proportions. That Cicero has not mentioned Antias because his style – *oratione sua* – did not match his (as Krause, p. 107, assumes), is an easy way out, which we will consider only if there is no other way; because Cicero was not someone who pretended that his opponents never existed. Hence, Cicero did not know Antias, and when we stay strictly with the Fragments, we find the following sure solution: For us, the *terminus post quem* is no longer in the year 91, the last year for which Antias's

---

[134]Macrobii, *Saturnalia*, 1.13.21; 1.16.32; Gellius, *Attic Nights*, 13.15.4.
[135]Cichorius, "Das Geschichtswerk des Sepronius Tuditanus", p. 588.
[136]Peter, *Historicorum Romanorum*, I, p. 146, Fragment 8.
[137]Plutarch, *Life of Cicero*, 9; Maximus, *Factorum et Dictorum Memorabilium*, 9.12.1; Peter, *Historicorum Romanorum reliquiae*.

fragments reports a particular event, but the year 51 in which Cicero published his work *De Legibus*, or rather the year 43, in which Cicero died. Because, in Cicero's lifetime, Antias's historical work barely was published. We only approximately can determine the *terminus ante quem* based on the lifetimes of Livy and Dionysius who mentioned him first for sure – approximately the year 30 BC. This conclusion seems to be without doubt.

There are also several important arguments that Antias's work was published between 44 and 30. Firstly, I must draw the attention to an essay of Holzapfel,[138] who associates Fragment 45 with an event of the year 73 by identifying the mentioned tribune of the people, Licinius, with the annalist Licinius Macer, who brought Gaius Rabirius[139] to court because

---

[138] Holzapfel, "ancora sull' etá di Valerio Antiate." *Rivista di storia antica e scienze affini* 4. Here, I must be content with the results of the essay that I found in the newest edition of Schanz, *Röm. Literaturgeschichte*, because I could not acquire the original essay. Because Münzer (*Hermes* 32, p. 46) simply declares the statements in the Fragments book 75, 74 and 45 as wrong (he arbitrarily replaces XLV with the number XV and LXXC with the number XXV) and – building on this assumption – assumes that the work in question was made up from at most 30 books, then this goes too far in the direction of hypothesis and does not deserve belief. And I do not agree with such a free treatment of the transmission. The same judgment must be applied to the assumption of Gutschmidt (Kleine Schriften, p. 527), who concludes the 22nd book with the death of Tiberius Gracchus and wants to assign one year for each book. He wants to associate the death of Sulla with the last book, and therefore assigns it the year 70. Münzer argues against him because the Fragment of book 45 allegedly contains the description of an event of the year 205. But Gutschmidt's hypothesis is brittle alone due to the fact that it builds on top of the following, fully unjust, premise: "it hardly can be assumed that the work reached into the Sullanistic time".

[139] Gaius Rabirius was a Roman senator who was involved in the death of Lucius Appuleius Saturninus in 100 BC. Titus Labienus, a Tribune of the Plebs whose uncle had lost his life among the followers of Saturninus on that occasion, was urged by fellow Senator and patron Julius Caesar to accuse Rabirius of participating in the murder. Caesar's real objective was to warn the Senate against interference by force with popular movements, to uphold the sovereignty of the people and the inviolability of the person of the tribunes, at the time of the conspiracy of Lucius Sergius Catilina. The obsolete accusation of *perduellio* was revived, and the case was heard before Caesar and his cousin Lucius Julius Caesar as commissioners specially appointed (*duumviri perduellionis*). Rabirius was condemned, and the people, to whom the accused had exercised the right of appeal, were on the point of ratifying the decision, when Quintus Caecilius Metellus Celer pulled down the military flag from the Janiculum, which was equivalent to the dissolution of the assembly. Cae-

of the desecration of holy places.[140] In Fragment 75, he also believes to have identified the funeral of Caesar and dates this work to after the year 44.

Now, I'd like to speak about the extent of his annals and afterwards use the biggest intact Fragment as proof that Valerius Antias is guilty of the anti-Caesarian falsifications [Ed.: which began a trend of fraudulent history that exists to this very day.]

Antias's story begins with the beginnings of Rome, and the second book further elaborates on the history of Numa Pompilius.[141] These portions dealing with the fabulous times of the kings are completely consonant with the character of the author, because on these topics, he could exercise his tendency to lie more and better regarding ancient times regarding which he could not easily be refuted. So, it is not unlikely that in his first book he went far afield and even elaborated on the Alban-kings. I note here that in the 22nd book he speaks about an event in the year 136.[142] Now, there are at least 53 books after book 22[143]; because Gellius mentions book 75 and this number is probably correct[144]; because Priscian mentions book 74. According to this, Antias would have needed 22 books to write the history up to the year 136, and at least another 50 books for the following time period of 70 years – if he, as is commonly believed, lived in the time of Sulla – i.e., even more volumes than Livy needed for the same time span. This improbability is reason enough to set his lifetime to a later point.

Antias's largest Fragment to which we have access[145] was addressed by Mommsen under the title of *Die Scipionenprozesse*. I cannot embark on a

---

sar's object having been attained, the matter was then allowed to drop. The defense was taken by Marcus Tullius Cicero, consul at the time; the speech is extant: *Pro Rabirio Reo Perduellionis*. See also: Dio 37.26–38. [Ed.]

[140] Cicero, *Pro Rabirius*, 2.7.
[141] Fragments 5 and 6.
[142] Gellius, *Attic Nights*, 6.9.17.
[143] However, in Fragment 15 we find that Antias tells about a decree of the Senate made in the year 181; that is probably a corruption because he otherwise would have needed one book from Numa until the year 181, and for the following 50 years, 21 books. Cf. Peter, *Historicorum Romanorum*: p. CCCVI, Note 2.
[144] Priscian 9, p. 489.
[145] Mommsen, *Römische Forschungen*, II, p. 419 sq.

closer inspection of this here; we have to be satisfied with his conclusion.[146]

After Mommsen clearly examined the legal issues and the general situation – as told by Polybius and Claudius Quadrigarius (as well as Cicero and Nepos) – he responds to the falsifications that can be found in Livy's reports. Due to a few particular points, it is clear that his main story is derived from Antias, because Livy mentions his name several times, at the beginning of the story (50.4), where he draws from another source (55.8), and at the end (59.2), where he again calls him by name.

[Editor's note: Here I will insert in Zohren's paper the story about how Publius Scipio and Lucius Scipio were accused of embezzlement. As he notes, this is, apparently, the largest fragment of the work of Antias that we have, and that thanks to Livy, to whom we now turn:

> Publius Scipio Africanus, as Valerius Antias asserts, was prosecuted by two men, each named Quintus Petillius. ... Some reproached, not the tribunes of the people, but the whole state, for being able to allow this – the two greatest cities in the world, they said, were at about the same time found ungrateful towards their foremost citizens, but Rome was more ungrateful, because conquered Carthage had driven the conquered Hannibal into exile, while victorious Rome was driving out the victorious Scipio. Others argued that no single citizen should attain such eminence that he could not be questioned under the law ... Against a man, they said, who cannot brook equitable law, no violence is illegal. (38.50.4–9)
>
> ... the tribunes revived the old charges of luxury in his winter-quarters at Syracuse ... they charged him with having accepted bribes ... he had been, they alleged, a dictator, not a lieutenant, in relation to the consul in the province ... that one man was the source and stay of Roman power, that under the shadow of Scipio the City which was the mistress of the world lay sheltered, that his nod was weighty as decrees of the Senate and enactments of the assembly. A man untouched by ill repute they loaded with innuendo in every possible way. (38.51.1–5)
>
> This was the last day of glory to shine on Publius Scipio ... He retired to his country place ... with the definite intention of not being present to plead his cause. His soul and character were too lofty, and too much accustomed to a greater fortune, to know how to be a defendant and to come down to the lowly position of men who

---

[146]Mommsen, "Die Scipionenprozesse", p. 493.

must plead their cause ... the tribunes who had accused him [refused to accept his refusal to plead his case and] maintained he had not come to plead ... because of arrogance ... those whom he had robbed of their right to express their opinion of him and of their liberty ... (37.52.1–5)

One of the tribunes of the people at this time was Tiberius Sempronius Gracchus, between whom and Publius Scipio there was a feud ... he had forbidden his name to be signed to the decree of his colleagues ... he thus decreed ... that he would not permit Publius Scipio to be prosecuted ... that he would come to Scipio's aid, to save him from pleading his cause: such heights had Publius Scipio reached, as a result of his own deeds and of the honours conferred by the Roman people, with the approbation of gods and men, that to compel him to stand as a defendant before the Rostra and listen to the insults of young men would be a greater disgrace to the Roman people than to Scipio himself. (38.52.8–11)

He supplemented his decree with an indignant speech: "Are your feet, tribunes, to trample down Scipio, that conqueror of Africa? Was it for this that he repulsed and routed four of the most noted generals of the Carthaginians in Spain, and four armies? ... Will you allow a victory over Publius Africanus to be sought? Shall distinguished men by no services of their own, by no honours of your bestowal, ever reach a safe and, as it were, sacred citadel where their old age, if not respected, at least secure, may find rest?"

Boundless gratitude was expressed by the whole order and especially by the senators of consular rank and greater age, because Tiberius Gracchus had shown greater regard for the public interest than for his personal quarrels, and the Petillii were assailed with abuse because they had tried to become conspicuous by darkening another's reputation and were seeking spoils from a triumph over Africanus. Thenceforth, there was silence regarding Africanus. He spent [the rest of] his life [in retirement] with no desire to return to the City ... when dying, they say that he gave orders that he should be buried in that same place in the country and ... that his funeral might not be held in an ungrateful home-land. (38.53, excerpts)

On the death of Africanus, the spirits of his adversaries rose, the first of them being Marcus Porcius Cato, who even during his life had been accustomed to snarl at his greatness. It was with his backing, it is thought, that the Petillii initiated the prosecution of Africanus while he lived and after his death introduced a motion. The motion was to this effect: "Do you wish and order, citizens, with respect to the money which was captured from, taken from, levied upon ... and what of this money has not been accounted for to the state, that ... the Senate wishes to investigate this mater ..." that the Senate should inquire regarding money which had not been turned in to the treasury in the manner in which it had always been done before. The Petillii kept assailing the influential position and tyrannical power of the Scipios in the Senate. ... Lucius Scipio ... complained that only after the death of his brother Publius Africanus, a man conspicuous above all for courage and fame, this proposal had originated; for it was not enough that no eulogy had been pronounced before the Rostra over Publius Africanus after his death without also bringing charges against him; even the Carthaginians had been satisfied with the exile of Hannibal, the Roman people was not content even with the death of Publius Scipio without also tearing to shreds his reputation as he lay in the tomb, and besides, sacrificing his brother as an additional victim to their jealousy. (38.54, excerpts)

Lucius Scipio was immediately arraigned ... These [extraordinary] amounts of gold and silver I have found recorded in the writings of Antias. In the case of Lucius Scipio, I should myself prefer to see an error of the scribe rather than a falsification of the historian in the amounts of gold and silver ...

At this point, Livy diverges from the account by Antias to bring forward other traditions.

... it is more probable that the fine assessed would have been 4 million rather than twenty-four million, the more so because there is a tradition that an accounting for just this sum was also demanded in the Senate from Publius Scipio himself, and that, when he had directed his brother Lucius to bring the account-book, he had himself, with his own hands, torn it up, being angry that after he had brought two hundred millions into the treasury he should be asked to account for four millions. With the same self-confidence, they say, when the quaestors did not dare to take money from the treasury contrary to the law, he demanded the keys and said that he would open the treasury who had brought it to pass that it was closed. (38.55)

Much else is said, especially about the end of Scipio's life, his trial, his death, his funeral, his tomb, all so contradictory that I find no tradition, no written documents, which I can accept. There is no unanimity as to his accuser: some say that Marcus Naevius accused him, others the Petillii; there is no agreement as to the time when he was prosecuted nor as to the year when he died nor as to where he died or was buried ... Not only is there disagreement among historians, but the speeches also (if indeed those which are in circulation are genuine works of these men) of Publius Scipio and Tiberius Gracchus are inconsistent with one another. ...

Another entirely different story must be put together, consistent with the oration of Gracchus, and those writers must be followed who say that, when Lucius Scipio was both accused and convicted of receiving money from the king, Africanus was serving on a commission in Etruria ... that he attacked [the tribunes] with more affection for his brother than respect for the laws. For it is just this conduct that Tiberius Gracchus complains of – that the tribunicial power had been infringed by a private citizen, and at the end, when he promised his official assistance to Lucius Scipio, he added that it seemed to be a more endurable precedent that a tribune of the people rather than a private citizen would have overthrown both the tribunicial power and the state. But this one act of uncontrolled violence on Scipio's part he loaded with reproaches ... [then] he paid him ... lasting and accumulated praises for his integrity and self-command; for he said that the people had once been rebuked by Scipio because they wished to make him perpetual consul and dictator; that he forbade statues to himself to be erected in the Comitium, on the Rostra, in the Curia, on the Capitoline, in the cell of Jupiter; that he prevented also a decree that his image in triumphal dress should appear to be coming out of the temple of Jupiter Optimus Maximus. (38.56)

However much at variance are these accounts of so great a man, they have seemed worthy of presentation. (38.57)

Here, Livy returns to the narrative based on Antias's recounting the trial and condemnation of Lucius Scipio and other lieutenants of Scipio Africanus. This tale gives ample opportunity to both subtly insult and to praise, though it must be said that the praise was of such a kind as to repel a Republican spirit.

> Publius Africanus had so far surpassed his father's praises that he had given reason to believe that he was born, not of human blood, but of divine stock. (38.58)

The end of the story is rather anti-climactic. After being condemned and almost being taken away in chains to prison because he could not pay the fine, Lucius was saved by the intervention of Tiberius Gracchus in a slightly different context than in the alternate story told by Livy above. Though all his property was confiscated, it was found that he had nothing of sufficient value to justify the accusation that he had absconded with millions in gold.

> Not only was there no trace of the king's wealth discovered, but by no means was there as much property found as would equal the amount of the fine. ... what was necessary for a decent existence was redeemed for him by his nearest relatives; and the ill-will against the Scipios ended by recoiling upon the heads of the praetor and his advisers and the accusers. (38.60)

Now, we return to Zohren's analysis. Editor's note end.]

Also Gellius enumerates the elements[147] where Antias differs from the older chronicles, and at the same moments we can find [Ed.: diversions] in the story of Livy. Therefore, the falsifications that can be discerned in Livy have to be 'booked' onto the account of Antias. They consist of a forceful implementation of something that the following transmission conveys: "that, what writers of historical novels justifiably do, and what historians, who revive the past, unjustifiably do."

That Livy mentions his source, Antias, so frequently, and repeatedly depends on him, must be attributed to the fact that Antias's account deviated markedly from other sources. Mommsen suspects that Livy could not find much about this [Ed.: legal] process [Ed.: against the Scipios] in his source Quadragarius, but in Antias, he found a lively, dramatic report. Thus, it is easily understandable why he preferred the account from Antias.

Now, within this legal prosecution we find two essays that, due to their anachronistic nature, are of particular interest to us. Especially the second one – which is said to have originated from Tiberius Gracchus – contains allusions and reminiscences that cannot possibly fit with Scipio. That only Caesar could have been hit by them has been evidenced by Mommsen, and because Scipio[148] was the first of the Roman commanders who showed 'Caesarian tendencies' it was not difficult for the contemporaries

---

[147] Gellius, *Attic Nights*, 6.19.8.
[148] Mommsen, *Römische Geschichte*, I, note 6, 630, 791, 824.

to identify the one who was being targeted, i.e., Caesar.[149] All of the following elements – Caesar's dictatorship for a lifetime,[150] the perpetuation of his consulate, the placement of his statues on the Rostra, in the Capitol and in the temple of Jupiter, the display of his image during festivities, the confiscation of cash after noncompliance with the tribunal powers, and all honours that were bestowed upon him in Rome and in the entire empire – [Ed.: rejected by Scipio, of course] – could move to outrage even the most lethargic Republicans. It was a lucky coincidence that the life of Scipio had parallels with Caesar's,[151] and so, the person/model of Scipio was used to damage the image and memory of Caesar himself.

Now, who originated this falsification? The whole other transmission about the "Scipionenprozesse" originates from Antias; but because his life was re-assigned to the time of Sulla, nobody cared to assign this essay to him. It must have been created after the year 44, and that is the reason why Nissen helped himself with the assumption that he was dealing with a declamantion of a school of rhetoric. Mommsen discards this hypothesis and perceives that this essay represents a skillful political pamphlet with a tendency to discredit Caesar. Mommsen reads from Livy himself that this essay was transmitted individually and not being part of the annals. Livy writes:

> *Index orationis P. Scipionis nomen M. Naevii tribuni plebis habet, ipsa oratio sine nomine est accusatoris.*

> The index of the speech of Publius Scipio contains the name of Marcus Naevius, tribune of the people; the speech itself lacks the name of the accuser ...[152]

But this obviously refers only to the first essay, i.e., of Publius Scipio against his accuser M. Raevius.

---

[149]It can also be noted that the intervention of Gracchus in a case where the accused was so clearly being depicted as "Caesarian" also ties the Gracchi and their reforms to Caesar; never mind that the Tiberius Gracchus involved with Scipio was the grandfather of the famous Gracchi reformers. [Ed.]

[150]Mommsen, *Corpus Inscriptionum Latinarum*, p. 462; Suetonius, *Ceasar*, 76; Drumann, *Geschichte Roms*, III, p. 663.

[151]Mommsen, *Römische Forschungen*, p. 502.

[152]Livy, *History of Rome*, 38.56.6.

We can understand that Livy and Gellius held doubts about their authenticity; because, according to Cicero's[153] explicit testimony,[154] there was no transmitted essay of Scipio. [Ed.: Here, Gellius's remarks on the topic:]

> How greatly the earlier Scipio Africanus excelled in the splendour of his merits, how lofty and noble of spirit he was, and to what an extent he was upheld by consciousness of his own rectitude, is evident from many of his words and acts. Among these are the following two instances of his extreme self-confidence and sense of superiority.
>
> When Marcus Naevius, tribune of the commons, accused him before the people and declared that he had received money from king Antiochus to make peace with him in the name of the Roman people on favourable and easy terms, and when the tribune added sundry other charges which were unworthy of so great a man, then Scipio, after a few preliminary remarks such as were called for by the dignity and renown of his life, said: "I recall, fellow citizens, that this is the day on which in Africa in a mighty battle I conquered Hannibal the Carthaginian, the most bitter enemy of your power, and won for you a splendid peace and a glorious victory. Let us then not be ungrateful to the gods, but, I suggest, let us leave this worthless fellow, and go at once to render thanks to Jupiter, greatest and best of gods." So saying, he turned away and set out for the Capitol. Thereupon the whole assembly, which had gathered to pass judgment on Scipio, left the tribune, accompanied Scipio to the Capitol, and then escorted him to his home with the joy and expressions of gratitude suited to a festal occasion. **The very speech is in circulation which is believed to have been delivered that day by Scipio, and those who deny its authenticity at least admit that these words which I have quoted were spoken by Scipio.**
>
> There is also another celebrated act of his. Certain Petilii, tribunes of the commons, influenced they say by Marcus Cato, Scipio's personal enemy, and instigated to appear against him, insisted most vigorously in the Senate on his rendering an account of the money of Antiochus and of the booty taken in that war; for he had been deputy to his brother Lucius Scipio Asiaticus, the commander in

---

[153] Cicero, *De Officiis*, 3.1.4.
[154] *Nulla eius ingenii monumenta mandata litteris, nullum opus otii, nullum solitudinis munus exstat.*

that campaign. Thereupon Scipio arose, and taking a roll from the fold of his toga, said that it contained an account of all the money and all the booty; that he had brought it to be publicly read and deposited in the treasury. "But that," said he, "I shall not do now, nor will I so degrade myself." And at once, before them all, he tore the roll across with his own hands and rent it into bits, indignant that an account of money taken in war should be required of him, to whose account the salvation of the Roman state and its power ought to be credited.[155]

But, this essay is of little interest for us here; because Livy does not quote from it – probably because it appeared to him as a normal literary forgery – but instead moves on to the essay of Tiberius Gracchus against Scipio without mentioning an *index* of it. This time, he quotes the essay, so we can assume that he has trusted it more than the others, and because he says: "*orationes P. Sciponis et Tib. Gracchi abhorrent inter se*" [the speeches ... P. Scipio and Tib. Gracchi, contain statements which are conflicting], and so the implied accusation would have gone mainly against the first essay; otherwise he would not have ignored the first essay, and quoted in detail the second essay.

After giving the content of the Gracchan speech in paragraph 56, he writes as follows at the beginning of 57:

> *Haec vel in laudatione posita ingentem magnitudinem animi moderantis ad civilem habitum honoribus significarent, quae exprobrando inimicus fatetur.*

> Such statements, even if included in a eulogy, would indicate the unusual greatness of a soul, which restricted distinctions to conformity with a democratic constitution, and they were made by an enemy and accompanied by censure.

Only someone who is certain that the previously reported discourse is accurate would act that way.

Now, I assume that Livy has taken the rest of the report from Antias and that he did not doubt its validity in the same way he did not doubt the rest of the picture; to me, it does not appear typical for this "puzzled and uncritical hasty-writer" – as Mommsen describes him – that he would

---

[155] Gellius, *Attic Nights*, 4.18.

stop in the middle of this dramatic story to suddenly begin a comparison of two transmitted essays of a later time. According to the perspective of Nitzsch,[156] Livy has never otherwise used more than one source for the same story, and while we can read in Dionysius[157] that he preferred the younger – more recent – annals because of their depth of details and because he could find numerous essays in them, would Livy not have found essays on such a dramatic scenario in Antias also? That appears to be more than unlikely, and it seems that this also was felt by Mommsen when he wrote: "T[his] essay corresponds to a better annalistic tradition." He was forced to help himself with the assumption of an [Ed.: anti-Caesar] pamphlet because he had the common firm belief that Antias lived during the time of Sulla and because it occurred to him that no other annalist could have been capable of such a falsification.

On the basis of the available transmitted materials I have proven extensively above that the long-assumed dates of the life of Antias must be disregarded; and we must presume that a historian of the ilk of Antias, who has pruned historical matters so ruthlessly and skillfully, would be equally skillful in inserting his own timeline into earlier history, thus striking at his opponents who did not share his political viewpoint. That Livy, a staunch Republican, recorded such sources without discernment, is not surprising since this essay of anti-Caesarian tendencies is a masterpiece of Antias.

Now [Ed.: having exposed Antias's level of cunning and subtlety] it is no longer difficult for us to connect other similar falsifications to him also, because other time periods were an even greater field of exploitation for him. We also can now completely exclude Tubero, especially when we consider that the name Antias appears 35 times in Livy,[158] whereas Tubero occurs only 3 times.

Coming back now to consideration of the Roman oath against kingship, there are various arguments regarding authorship of the oath by Antias. It hardly can be doubted that he is the main source, if not the only source,

---

[156] Nitzsch, *Römische und deutsche Annalistik und Geschichtschreibung. Eine kritische Parallele*, p. 272.
[157] Ibid., p. 171.
[158] Cf. Peter, *Historicorum Romanorum*; Nissen, *Kritische Untersuchungen über die Quellen der vierten und fünften Dekade des Livius*, p. 44.

in Plutarch's *Publicola*.¹⁵⁹ That is the reason why it is that in this source we find the version wherein it is attempted to justify and involve the whole Senate. That Antias was used for this account also follows from the fact that in Plutarch, Valerius Publicola takes the oath first, thereby subtracting a bit from the credit and glory of Brutus. [Ed.: This is a significant indicator of the identity of the falsifier who sought to bring glory to his own gens.]

The first writer who cited the existence of this oath, unknown to Cicero and those before him, must have been Asinius Pollio, whom Appian used as his source almost exclusively.¹⁶⁰ Pollio's historical work appeared around the year 30. It is not certain if he elaborated beyond the times of the Battle of Philippi, but he must still have dealt with the dispute between Antonius and the murderers of Caesar. When Tacitus says about him: "*Asinii Pollionis scripta egregiam eorundem (sc. Cassii et Bruti) memoriam tradunt*" [Asinius Pollio has written a glorious account of them],¹⁶¹ it is natural that he didn't leave himself open to be accused of memorializing individuals who had made a false oath to protect Caesar and therefore was obliged to mention the prior oath of the ancient Romans as the protective mechanism. The mention of this was very short in Appian, but by that time, everybody obviously knew about the meaning of it, and the tale of the ancient oath had taken hold to such an extent that Livy and Dionysius incorporated it without a second thought. Antias's popularity¹⁶² had enabled a wide dissemination of the story; due to his addiction to win readers by publishing the new and the outrageous, he had managed to achieve the exceptional amongst the younger writers.

The situation is even clearer in the *lex Valerius Publicolae*. According to Münzer¹⁶³ in the history of Piso, the Valerius was not presented in a very

---

[159] Kießling, *Dionysi Halicarnasensis Antiquitatum Romanarum quae supersunt*, p. 24; Peter, *Quellen Plutarchs in den Biographien der Römer*, p. 24; Münzer, *De gente Valeria*, p. 909.

[160] cf. Mommsen, *Corpus Inscriptionum Latinarum*, Appian p. 229; Drumann, *Geschichte Roms*, II.1-42, 1 not. Thouret, *De Cicerone Asinio Pollione C Oppio: Rerum Caesarianarum Scriptoribus*, p. 324; Hinz, *Zur Beurteilung Asinios und Plutarchs*.

[161] Tacitus, *Annals*, 4.34.

[162] Nitzsch, *Römische und deutsche Annalistik und Geschichtschreibung. Eine kritische Parallele*, p. 186.

[163] The reason for Münzer's suspicion may be found in his publication on p. 14.

favorable light; as a Patrician, he had aspired to kingship but dropped the undertaking in a moment of danger to regain the goodwill of the populace which had come to hate him. Münzer may have gone too far with this statement. But the historical tradition, taken as a whole, demonstrates that the ancient Valerius Publicola did not always demonstrate a Republican disposition.[164][165] There exists also some disagreement over Publicola's attempts to silence all suspicions about his regnal intentions. One explanation could be that historians – due to dislike of the Valerians – have only focused and expanded upon the negative sides of Valerius Publicola. Piso was certainly one of them.

Without question then, Antias has eagerly endeavored to remove all guilt from his alleged progenitor, and he indeed has managed to portray him to a naive audience as a liberator of the homeland, as a lawful founder of the Republic. He obviously imputed to him more glorious aspects, and Livy alludes to that when he begins with "*ante omnes*",[166] without touching the other things. It was not easy to connect the authorship of the foundational laws of the Republic with Publicola, since it should have originated from Brutus. But – he must have asked himself – why not additionally create a pre-existing law that rendered such exquisite benefits to the murderers of Caesar? It was entirely possible and he also could glorify his family with it, which was the most important thing in his work. At the same time, it was very easy to find the template for the law in the *leges Horatiae Valeriae*, which guaranteed the perpetuity of the *provocatio* by the enactment that "no one should in future create a magistrate from whom there was no appeal; anyone who created such a magistrate should be protected by no law, sacred of profane, and might be slain with impunity." It was P. Valerius who allegedly proposed this law to relieve himself from the suspicion of aiming at kingship, but the big question is: did it really happen? Or did Antias make up that story as well?

As noted above, Livy states that the Valerian law was enacted again, for the third time, in 299 BC. Livy notes that in all three cases the law was

---

[164]So again, we see then hand of Valerius Antias rehabilitating his ancestor. [Ed.]

[165]cf. Schwegler, *Römische Geschichte*, p.283; Niebuhr, *Römische Geschichte*, I.4, p. 564; Ihne, *Römische Geschichte*, I, p. 107; Ihne, *Forschungen auf dem Gebiete der römischen Verfassungsgeschichte*, p. 42.

[166]Livy, *History of Rome*, 2.8.2.

enacted by a member of the Valerius family. However, the ancient history of the kings suggests that the original right of appeal emerged from them, not from the early Republic and that is, perhaps, why the law includes the term *Horatiae*. During the reign of Tullus Hostilias (approx. 672–642 BC), the trial of Horatius for killing his sister, betrothed to a man he had just killed in a battle, took place. For the murder, he was condemned to death, but upon the advice of either the king – who did not want to condemn him though he was bound by his own laws to do so – or a certain jurist named Tullus, Horatius appealed to the assembly of the people. Horatius's father, also called Publius, spoke to the people of his son's recent victory, and entreated them not to render him childless since he had, until recently, had four children. Persuaded by his father's arguments, the people acquitted Horatius.[167] This legend is the more likely origin of the right of *provocatio*, but the terms could be retroactively utilized.

Thus, it appears that Antias, utilizing the same template of a preexisting law upheld by a holy vow, strove cunningly to rehabilitate not only his ancestor, but the murderers of Julius Caesar as well.

---

[167] Livy, *History of Rome*, 1.24–26.

Bibliography

Appian. *Civil Wars.*
Badian, Ernst. *Studies in Greek and Roman History.* Blackwell's Oxford, 1964.
Beard, Mary. "Spinning Caesar's murder: Putting the ideology – and the people – back into our understanding of Roman political life". In: *Times Literary Supplement* (May 13, 2009).
Caesar. *Civil War.*
Canfora, Luciano. *Julius Caesar: The People's Dictator.* Edinburgh University, 1999.
Cicero. *Academica.*
— *Ad Atticum.*
— *Ad Familiares.*
— *Ad Quintum Fratrem.*
— *De Haruspicum Responso.*
— *De Legibus.*
— *De Officiis.*
— *De Re Publica.*
— *De Senectute.*
— *Fragments.*
— *Philippica.*
— *Pro C. Rabirio perduellionis reo.*
— *Pro Rabirius.*
— *Rhetorica ad Herennium.* Trans. by Harry Caplan. Loeb Classical Library No. 403, 1954.
Cichorius. "Das Geschichtswerk des Sepronius Tuditanus". In: *Wiender Studien* 24 (1902).
Cornell, Tim J. *Fragments of the Roman Historians.* Vol. 1. Oxford University Press, 2013.
Dio, Cassius. *Roman History.*
Dionysius. *Roman Antiquities.*
Drumann, Wilhelm. *Geschichte Roms.* Gebrüder Bornträger, 1834.
Forsythe, Gary. *A Critical History of Early Rome: From Prehistory to the First Punic War.* University of California Press, 2006.
Fronto. *Epistula ad Verum.*
Gellius, Aulus. *Attic Nights.*

Gorman, Vanessa B., Eric W. Robinson, and A. J. Graham, eds. *Oikistes: Studies in Constitutions, Colonies, and Military Power in the Ancient World, Offered in Honor of A.J. Graham*. Mnemosyne Supplements, Book 234. Brill Academic Publishers, Sept. 1, 2002.

Hinz, G. *Zur Beurteilung Asinios und Plutarchs.*

Ihne, Wilhelm. *Forschungen auf dem Gebiete der römischen Verfassungsgeschichte.* Frankfurt am Main: Hermann Johann Kessler, 1847.

— *Römische Geschichte.* Leipzig: Wilhelm Engelmann, 1890.

Kahn, Arthur D. *The Education of Julius Caesar: A Biography, a Reconstruction.* Backinprint.Com, 1986.

Kießling, Adolf. *Dionysi Halicarnasensis Antiquitatum Romanarum quae supersunt.*

Krause, August. *Vitae Et Fragmenta Veterum Historicorum Romanorum.*

Lange, Ludwig. *Römische Altertümer.* Berlin: Weidmannsche Buchhandlung, 1862.

Liebaldt, Hermann. *De Valerio Antiate, annalium scriptore.* 1840.

Livy. *History of Rome.*

Macrobii. *Saturnalia.*

Marx, Friedrich. *Rhetorica ad Herennium.* Leipzig: Tuebner, 1894.

Maximus, Valerius. *Factorum et Dictorum Memorabilium.*

Mommsen, Theodor, ed. *Corpus Inscriptionum Latinarum.* 1853.

— "Die Scipionenprozesse". German. In: *Hermes* 1.H. 3 (1866), pp. 161–216. URL: http://www.jstor.org/stable/4470944.

— *Römische Forschungen.* Weidmannsche Buchhandlung, 1864.

— *Römische Geschichte.* Berlin: Weidmannsche Buchhandlung, 1856.

— *Römisches Staatsrecht.* Hirzel, 1876.

— *Römisches Strafrecht.* Leipzig: Duncker Humblot, 1899.

Münzer, Friedrich. *Beiträge zur Quellenkritik der Naturgeschichte des Plinius.* Berlin: Weidmannsche Buchhandlung, 1897.

— *De gente Valeria.* 1891.

Napoleon. *Histoire de Jules César.* 1865.

Niebuhr, Barthold Georg. *Römische Geschichte.* Berlin: Reimer, 1836.

Nipperdey, Thomas. "Zur Geschichte der röm. Historiographie". German. In: *Philol.* 6 (1851).

Nissen, Heinrich. *Kritische Untersuchungen über die Quellen der vierten und fünften Dekade des Livius.* Berlin: Weidmannsche Buchhandlung, 1863.

Nitzsch, Karl Wilhelm. *Römische und deutsche Annalistik und Geschichtschreibung. Eine kritische Parallele.* Historische Zeitschrift.

Pauly, August Friedrich and Georg Wissowa, eds. *Realencyclopädie der Classischen Altertumswissenschaft.* 1893-1978.

Peter, Hermannus. *Historicorum Romanorum.*

— *Historicorum Romanorum reliquiae.*

— *Quellen Plutarchs in den Biographien der Römer*.
Pliny. *Natural History*.
Plutarch. *Life of Cicero*.
— *Life of Publicola*.
Schmidt, Otto Eduard. *Römisches Strafrecht*. Leipzig: B. G. Teubner, 1893.
Schwegler, Albert. *Römische Geschichte*. 1853-1858.
Seeck, Otto. "Der Bericht des Livius über den Winter 218/17 v. Chr." German. In: *Hermes* 8 (1874), pp. 152–166. URL: http://w3d.digizeitschriften.de/main/dms/img/?PPN=PPN509862098_0008&DMDID=dmdlog23.
Smith, William. *Dictionary of Greek and Roman Biography and Mythology*. Leipzig: B. G. Teubner, 1870.
Stelkens. "Der Römische Geschichtsschreiber Sempronius Asellio". German. In: *Progr. Krefeld* (1887).
Suetonius. *Ceasar*.
Tacitus. *Annals*.
Thouret, Georgius. *De Cicerone Asinio Pollione C Oppio: Rerum Caesarianarum Scriptoribus*. 1878.
Velleius Paterculus. *Roman History*.
Wiseman, Timothy Peter. *Roman drama and Roman history*. University of Exeter Press, 1998.

Index

Accius, 62
Acilius, 66
Aeneas, 32
Africanus, 59, 66, 71–74, 77
Ahala, 36, 43, 48, 49
Albucius, 61
Antias, 1, 9–11, 18, 20, 31, 57–64, 66, 68–71, 73–76, 78–82
Antipater, 18, 66
Antonius, 40–42, 80
Appian, 32, 34, 35, 41, 44, 57, 67, 80
Asellio, 66
Aufidius, 66
Augustus, 7, 31, 35
Aurelius, 60

Brutus, 10, 31–35, 37–40, 43, 49, 66, 80, 81

Caesar, 1, 7–9, 11–18, 22, 23, 26, 27, 31, 34, 35, 38–44, 47, 48, 52–56, 61, 69, 70, 75, 76, 79–82
Capitolinus, 36
Carus, 61
Cassius, 31, 32, 36, 45, 66, 67
Cato, 7, 65, 68, 72, 77
Cicero, 1, 7–10, 22–26, 31, 32, 36–39, 45, 46, 48–50, 52, 55, 56, 60–62, 65–71, 77, 80
Clodius, 17, 66
Collatinus, 33, 37

Dionysius, 31, 33–36, 43–45, 47, 50, 57, 64, 65, 67–69, 79, 80

Ennius, 38, 62, 65

Fabius, 48, 65, 66, 68
Flaminius, 51
Fronto, 60, 61

Gellius, 60, 66, 70, 75, 77
Germanicus, 32
Gracchus, 14, 17, 51, 66, 67, 69, 72, 74–76, 78

Hemina, 66, 67
Herennius, 38
Horatius, 82
Hostilias, 82
Hyginus, 63

Jugurthen, 59

Krause, 64, 68

Lepidus, 41
Licinius, 20, 57, 66, 68, 69
Liebaldt, 64
Livy, 11, 31–36, 39, 40, 44, 46–50, 52, 53, 57–59, 64, 66, 67, 69–71, 73–81
Lucretinus, 61

Macer, 20, 57, 66, 68, 69
Maelius, 36, 45, 48–51
Manlius, 36, 45, 57
Marius, 25, 59, 60
Maximus, 31, 49, 63, 66, 68, 74
Mommsen, 9, 12, 18, 31, 35, 36, 39, 47, 48, 50, 70, 71, 75, 76, 78, 79

Octavian, 7, 41
Oppius, 56

Pacuvius, 61
Paterculus, 58, 60
Peter, 57, 59–63, 65, 67, 70
Pictor, 48, 60, 61, 65, 66
Piso, 48, 50, 65, 68, 80, 81
Plutarch, 31, 34, 35, 44, 45, 47, 57, 80
Pollio, 11, 80
Polybius, 18, 22, 38, 66, 71
Pompeius, 32, 56, 61
Pompilius, 70
Postumius, 66
Publicola, 31, 35, 36, 44–46, 48, 80, 81

Quadrigarius, 20, 58–60, 62, 66, 71
Quinctius, 49, 50

Rabirius, 69

Rutilius, 58

Sallust, 32, 61, 66
Scipio, 39, 52, 58, 59, 61, 66, 70–78
Seeck, 51, 52
Sejanus, 59
Servilius, 36, 43, 48–51
Sisenna, 18, 19, 58, 59, 61, 62, 66, 68
Suetonius, 40, 44, 56
Sulla, 18, 39, 47, 58–60, 69, 70, 76, 79
Sulpicius, 57

Tarquinius, 32–34, 36, 37, 52–55
Tiberius, 32, 59, 69, 72, 74–76, 78
Tubero, 56, 57, 79
Tuditanus, 66–68

Varro, 19, 20, 62–64, 67
Velleius, 58, 59, 61
Vennonius, 65
Verus, 60
Vinicius, 59

www.ingramcontent.com/pod-product-compliance
Lightning Source LLC
Chambersburg PA
CBHW070937160426
43193CB00011B/1724